M000223224

Book 3

WITNESSING THE HOLOCAUST

The Dutch in Wartime
Survivors Remember

Edited by

Tom Bijvoet

Mokeham Publishing Inc.

© 2012, 2013 Mokeham Publishing Inc.
PO Box 35026, Oakville, ON L6L 0C8, Canada
PO Box 559, Niagara Falls, NY 14304, USA
www.mokeham.com

Cover photograph by Bert Kaufmann

ISBN 978-0-9868308-4-6

Contents

This camp
is in
Drente –
Very
worthwhile
visit. Anne
Frank stayed
here before
going to Germany

On the front cover

The 102,000 Bricks monument, of which a detail is shown on the cover, commemorates the 102,000 people that were incarcerated in Westerbork Transit Camp and did not survive the war.

102,000 red bricks are put in the ground short side up on a large map of The Netherlands. On top of 213 of the bricks is a metal flame, these bricks represent Roma and Sinti (Gypsy) victims. 54 undecorated bricks represent the resistance fighters who were executed and cremated in the camp. All the other bricks have a metal Star of David. These represent the more than 101,000 Jewish inmates who were deported to their deaths in Auschwitz, Sobibor and other concentration camps.

The idea behind the 102,000 bricks is to visualize how many people were murdered. But in addition to the mass nature of the crime the monument illustrates, by using different height bricks, the individuality of the victims: 102,000 is not just a number, it is 102,000 unique human beings.

Designed by J.A. Gilbert and P.A. Ritmeijer, the monument was unveiled in 1992 by Her Royal Highness Princess Margriet of the Netherlands.

Introduction

Tom Bijvoet

They did not return would have been as appropriate a title for this book as the one we have chosen. In memory after memory of the forcible and violent removal of the Jewish population of The Netherlands, that is what we read: they did not return. The hard figures are indeed stark and chilling and underline that simple sentence. No numbers about the mass murder of Dutch Jewry can ever be entirely accurate, but of the 140,000 Jews who lived in the country in 1939 about 120,000 were deported to concentration camps and death camps in Germany and Poland, 102,000 of them were killed. That represents a devastatingly high percentage when contrasted with neighboring countries. Many reasons have been postulated about why that may have been the case and this is not the place to repeat that particular discussion. Suffice it to say that 'they did not return' accurately describes what happened.

When I grew up in The Netherlands in the 1960s the war was everywhere. Society had been defined by it. All adults around me had lived through those devastating war years. From them I heard stories about the sense of betrayal and shock at the start of the war, about the terror of the occupying Nazis, about hidden radios, random raids to round up young men for work in Germany, confiscated bicycles, brave acts of defiance and resistance, rationing, soup kitchens, famine and death by hunger in that last, devastating winter of the war and of course about the elation of liberation and freedom from oppression in 1945. Stories similar to the ones that are collected in this series of books, which was initiated by the authors of these stories themselves: 'publish them, before we die and cannot tell them anymore' they said. But I heard very few first-hand accounts of the persecution of the Jews in Holland, the people who could have told these stories had not returned.

When I think back on those days of my early youth, however hard I try, I remember only two people who had some connection with the Holocaust. The mother of a friend of mine was Jewish. She had survived the war by hiding on a farm in the village where I lived and after the war she had married the farmer's son. The second, a colleague of my father and a family friend, was half Jewish. His Jewish mother had survived the war, but most of his family, including his grandparents did not return. He did not speak to us about that.

This is not to say of course that we did not hear about the Holocaust, a term that we did not know yet at that time. The 'persecution of Jews' as we knew it was part of the curriculum. We read Anne Frank's diary. We were shown at a tender young age the iconic, traumatizing pictures of the concentration camps after their liberation. The piles of clothes, glasses, shoes. The piles of bodies. The emaciated inmates in their barracks. The images that have defined the Holocaust for the whole world and made us all witnesses to this worst crime ever committed. But we did not hear first-hand stories as we did about all the other atrocities of World War II.

Nevertheless the stories exist. Many have been told. Do we need more stories? After Anne Frank, after Etty Hillesum, after Primo Levi, after Elie Wiesel, after those shocking film reels. Dutch-American poet Leo Vroman concluded his poem 'Peace' with the following famous lines:

Let the stories tonight be told
Of how the war has disappeared
And repeat them hundredfold
Every single time I'll weep.

Yes, we need the stories. Six million stories disappeared of which 102,000 in The Netherlands. Six million individual stories. We should cherish the few that the surviving witnesses can tell us. This little book contains sixteen of them. No, the authors of these small histories did not peek through a viewing hole into a gas chamber in operation, as apparently Heinrich Himmler did when he visited Sobibor to 'celebrate' - what an impossible word - a milestone in the number of Jews gassed. But they saw trains heading east, they saw Jewish neighbors being dragged from their homes, they hid Jews in their houses, or in a few cases they survived concentration camps. The authors of the stories in this book witnessed aspects of the Holocaust that help, memory by memory, victim by victim, tell the story of 102,000 Dutch Jews, 102,000 individuals as is so evocatively symbolized by the monument shown on the cover of this book, who did not return. And just to make that a little more tangible, if that is possible, you would need between 700 and 800 copies of this book, side by side, to represent the full magnitude of the crime committed against the Dutch Jews alone. Make that an already unimaginable 40,000 to 50,000 copies for the entire Holocaust.

I wish to thank the authors who have been willing to dig into, in many cases, a traumatic past and to share with us their stories. Stories that need to be told.

Historical background

The Netherlands had long been a safe haven for Jewish people. From the persecuted Spanish and Portuguese Jews who fled the Inquisition in the early 16th century, to the latest group to have reached the Netherlands, the German Jews escaping Nazi persecution next door, Anne Frank and her family among them. The thoroughly assimilated Dutch Jews were unaccustomed to the harsh realities of the severe breed of anti-Semitism that was more prevalent in Eastern Europe and that had been institutionalized under the Nazis in Germany by the time neutral Holland was invaded.

Approximately 140,000 Jews lived in the Netherlands when the country was invaded in May of 1940. 75 Percent of those 140,000 people did not survive the Shoah, the Holocaust, the Catastrophe or as the Germans put it: the Final Solution to the Jewish question.

It did not take long after the invasion until the Germans implemented their first anti-Jewish measures. On July 1st, 1940 Jews were barred from membership in the civil air defense, in September the Civil Service was banned from hiring any more Jews and in October all civil servants had to sign a statement declaring they were 'Aryans', culminating in the dismissal in November of all Jewish civil servants. Serious measures to be sure, but not mass-murder. And therein lay the poisonous nature of the occupiers' approach. Gradually, almost imperceptibly, they hoped, the Jews could be isolated from the rest of the Dutch people. The final destruction could then take place without significant opposition.

New measures continued to be introduced: January 1941, all Jews have to register with the authorities; March, a German administrator is appointed in all Jewish-owned corporations; May, all Jews have to hand in their radios; September, Jewish children have to go to separate Jewish schools; also in September, the hated signs with 'no entry for Jews' go up in parks, zoos, pubs, restaurants, hotels, theaters, cinemas, sports facilities, libraries and museums.

In the meantime the first raids had started. Angered by regular disturbances in Amsterdam, where Jewish youths had decided to fight back, a raid took place in the districts in Amsterdam where a high concentration of Jews lived. 427 Young Jewish men were rounded-up and sent to Mauthausen Concentration Camp in Austria. Most succumbed under the cruelty of the regime within days. By the end of the year every single one of them was dead. Several more round-ups took place in 1941 in Amsterdam and the provinces of Gelderland and Overijssel.

Early in 1942 the Germans continue their policy of isolating the Jews by forcing them to move into specifically designated areas of Amsterdam. Measures, too many to exhaustively list, continued to be introduced. Among them a ban on driving a car, using a phone, fishing, participating in any sports, visiting a barber and bicycling. In May all Jews had to sew a bright yellow Star of David onto their clothes and were forbidden to appear in public without it clearly showing.

'Jewish Transit' camp Westerbork in the north of the country was outfitted as a temporary 'holding tank' for Jews being sent east. Initially Jews were told when to take a deportation train to Westerbork, but soon highly organized, often violent, round-ups took place at night in the areas where the Germans had forcibly concentrated the Jewish residents of The Netherlands. The Nazi authorities were aided in their persecution of the Jews by the highly sophisticated and meticulously kept Dutch civil registry. The registry contained details, including name, address and religion of everyone in the country. The registry was linked to the mandatory photo identification cards that everyone had to carry and show whenever ordered to do so. A large J was stamped on the IDs of Jewish cardholders for ease of recognition during the constant random ID-card inspections on public transit, at road-blocks, in theaters, at sports-matches or wherever the authorities thought they might have a good chance of catching Jews who had not voluntarily joined their assigned deportation train, resistance workers, or people otherwise living a life on the run.

In July of 1942 the first train with 1137 people on board left from Westerbork for Auschwitz. In the next two years more than sixty trains would follow this first transport to Auschwitz. Nineteen trains would go to Sobibor with 34,313 people on board of whom just 18 survived. About ten trains in total went to Belsen and Theresienstadt.

Although everyone knew that whatever awaited the deportees in the East was not going to be pleasant, the real truth, the mass slaughter, was too terrible to believe, or even comprehend. That is why so many got on the trains so peacefully.

Some 25,000 Jews went into hiding. Many more may have wanted to do the same, but lacked the contacts or the funds that were often required. Groups within the Resistance dedicated themselves to such tasks as finding safe accommodation, moving people around, forging ID-cards, acquiring or forging ration cards and collecting funds for food and lodging. Several thousand of the people who went into hiding were eventually caught, through betrayal, carelessness, or random raids on potential hiding places. When caught immediate deportation or in some cases execution on the spot took place. The people hiding the Jews ran serious risks themselves and faced potential deportation to German prisons or concentration camps.

In February of 1944 the last Jews were rounded up in Amsterdam, and with the exception of those who had gone into hiding and had not been caught, Holland was, as the Nazis had planned, 'clean of Jews'.

Brutally tormented, physically wrecked and mentally traumatized, about 5,000 Jewish deportees returned after the war to empty and plundered neighborhoods, a decimated circle of relatives and friends, and a shockingly unwelcome reception by the Dutch authorities.

Map: Concentration Camps

Netherlands
Westerbork
Neuengamme
Bergen-Belsen
Amsterdam
Vught
Berlin
Germany
Warsaw
Poland
Sobibor
Theresienstadt
Prague
Czech Rep.
Auschwitz
Mauthausen
Vienna
Austria

322 Kilometers
200 Miles

O Capital City
O Concentration Camp
mentioned in the text

Countries shown
with current borders

The map above shows the location of the concentration camps mentioned in the text. For ease of identification the map is shown with current national borders.

I never saw her again

Christina Sobole-van der Kroon

I was 17 years old in 1939 and found work in a sweatshop called Jansen & Neumann. My job was to sew buttons onto heavy dark green uniforms for the Dutch army, eight buttons in two rows. To make some money one had to work fast and good. How proud I was with my first self-earned money, 32 guilders, because I had indeed worked fast and good.

Early one morning in May of the next year my mother came into our bedroom and spoke the words: "children, children, there's war," all the while clapping her hands to wake the seven of us up. I will never forget that day, because I had a dental appointment that morning.

Soon after at work we were ordered to continue to make uniforms, but now for the German army. The same heavy dark green uniforms with the same rows of buttons.

During that time we lived in the Jewish district of Amsterdam, near Waterloo Square (Waterlooplein). We witnessed how Jews were pushed onto trucks with only a pillowcase of belongings on their backs.

Jewish people had to wear a yellow Star of David on their clothes in order to work and live. There were frequent round-ups of Jews in the neighborhood, which was very frightening.

At that point I was angry and I knew I had to make a decision. I should either quit work or stay and rebel silently. We needed the money, so I stayed. I planned to sabotage the German army. I continued to sew on the buttons, but in such a way that by closing the uniforms the buttons would jump off the uniform and the soldiers would have to fight with open and flapping uniforms. 'That is no way to win a war,' I thought naively.

There was a Jewish girl I worked with and I grew fond of her. Her name was Liesje Brandon. Her family was sent off to a concentration camp, she did not know which one, and Liesje was all alone and scared without a family. Then one morning she handed me a suitcase and said: "I am going to find my parents, because I cannot live without them anymore." She left and I never saw her again.

My father told me to take the stars off her clothes and to put the suitcase in the attic. After the war when Liesje did not return the suitcase was destroyed.

I am writing this mainly to honor a very brave courageous girl, Liesje Brandon.

My street

Anne Bourne

In memory of Anki, Rodi, Samu,
Freekje, Sam and all the others...

My life as a 12-year old was good. School was a happy place where I was with all my friends. After school we played together in our street, or indoors when the weather was bad. We often went to the nearby beach and we went roller skating in the big parking-lot there in the off-season.

Then one morning, very early, my mother woke my brother and me. She told us to get up because as she said, "there's war"! We stood at the windows in our pajamas, the sky was still dark. We saw planes in the distance; one came down burning! We could hear the anti-aircraft guns: 'plop, plop, plop'!

When it got lighter, at the front of our home some people went outside. Dutch soldiers came, they urged the people to go back inside. They then stood watch at both ends of our street. A little later my mother and I went out to do some shopping. Some planes came over really low and I saw the big black cross on their wings: Germans! Air raid sirens sounded and we stayed in the butchers shop until the sirens came on again in a steady drone as signal that it was safe to come out!

After 5 days of active war, our army capitulated and we went back to school. Initially everything seemed just like before. But gradually the German occupation took hold. After a while their directives seemed mostly aimed at Jewish people.

I asked myself: who was Jewish? We all seemed to lead the same lives. We kids never talked about religion, that was just not interesting! Our world was that of Deanna Durbin, Shirley Temple, Tarzan and the Dionne Quintuplets! But yes, there were some Jewish people who observed their religion. I knew the old man who had the candy shop was Jewish, because he always wore a black hat and had a beard! My friend, Willy, told me that she was Israelite, and that seemed better than Jewish, suddenly!

We knew Samu, a boy in our street, was really Jewish. On Saturdays, his 'Sunday,' he wore a nice suit and a tie. He would stand on the side, not daring to join our games afraid of dirtying his suit!

To us we were all Dutch children and that was it - all the same! Then, one day, our friends had to wear a yellow star on their clothes with the word 'Jew' in it. We started to feel separated, that was not good. But we accepted it together and we continued our lives together as always. But a new word I learned was, 'Aryan'. What was that?

Then my friends were forbidden to go to just any shop. They had to go to Jewish-owned stores and only between certain hours! That was inconvenient, of course.

My best friends, Rodi and Anki, spoke to me about going to Palestine. I had not heard much about that, but they seemed to like the idea. I just felt they were Dutch and should stay with us! But then they were ordered to go to Jewish schools! I thought that was terrible, they had to leave me? We always walked to school together, went to the same gymnastics club. We could not play handball in the park anymore. Before, when we played near the boardwalk we all ran back to our street together and we poked fun at the differences and laughed together! We could no longer do that. Gradually our lives had taken different directions! They had a curfew, they had to be inside at 8 p.m. We still played indoors together, even though that was also forbidden.

Then the words, 'work-camps in Poland' appeared. Some Jewish fathers, like Mr. Gobes across the street, had already disappeared somewhere. Youngsters of about sixteen were called up. Then some families suddenly disappeared during the night! My brother called me in the morning and told me: "Willy has gone to Switzerland!" She had only told him about it, then she disappeared! Some took the Southern route to Spain via Belgium and France. So went Samu, his parents and 5 children, but they were caught in Belgium. Later on, after the war, we heard they died in Auschwitz on August 31, 1942, all of them.

Our Jewish friends told us about the Jewish Council! You could get extensions to stay in Holland, instead of being sent to the work-camps. But you needed to take papers to the Jewish Council. How were you to do that, if you did not even have a bicycle and you were not allowed in the streetcar? So my brother, all of 15 years old, still wearing the short pants for a boy of his age, offered to go by streetcar. And he did! What came out of it, I guess, was not much, but he tried!

It was hot and sunny one day in July of 1942, when we heard some heavy trucks entering our street about dinner-time. We opened the windows wider and we leaned out to see what was happening. We saw two army trucks and several German soldiers with guns over their shoulders. Some took up positions at intervals on the sidewalks and other went to specific addresses.

They knew exactly where to go, to the Jewish families.

Mrs. Gobes leaned out of one of her windows across the street. She cried and cried and desperately asked, "What can I do?" We called out, "go to bed, act as if you are ill!" She did that, but when the Germans went to her house she appeared sometime later with her two children, Freekje and Sammy. Sammy appeared to be happy, finally being able to carry the Red Cross first aid kit, which he had just received as a birthday present. Mrs. Gobes softly cried when she went to the truck. We tried to go across the street to say goodbye, but a soldier held us back. So we called out softly, "Bon voyage". What else could we say? The whole truck was very quiet and so were we. We stood there until the German soldier told us to go inside. So we did. We were just as bewildered as our friends: Why?

Later we found out that my friends Anki and Rodi, had also been taken away with their parents. They were identical twins, but because I saw them nearly every day I could tell them apart. I went to their house the next day and saw their two identical summer dresses at the back of the house fluttering in the wind, hanging from the balcony.

Anki and Rodi and their parents, died in Auschwitz on September 7, 1942.

Mr. Gobes died on October 31, 1942 also in Auschwitz. His family died on September 17, 1942.

Samu, one of the 5 children died with the rest of his family on August 31, 1942.

These details were given to me at the synagogue in Amsterdam. I heard this after the war when I asked about my friends, my dear friends. Kaddish.

Suzanne's Star

Art van Leeuwen

I was born in a fishing town called IJmuiden a mile away from the North Sea. During the summer months before the war started my parents sent me to visit and stay with Uncle Tony who lived in Germany. I was about twelve years old at the time. Uncle Tony worked for a restaurant equipment company and he would send me along with some of the drivers as a helper.

As we traveled through the country I could see Germany preparing for war. We would encounter many military trucks and transports. In the skies above you could see aircraft engaged in flying exercises. I remember finding it very unsettling. I had learned German at school so I could read the signs on the side of the road. There were propaganda signs attacking the Jewish people with hateful statements and phrases I knew not to be true. I remember being upset and disgusted.

In IJmuiden there were three sets of locks that ships on their way to and from Amsterdam have to pass through. Fishing boats from different countries such as Denmark, Belgium, England and Norway would make their way through the locks. My dad worked where they unloaded the fish from the boats. We always had fresh fish.

When the Germans invaded many Jewish people came to the market in IJmuiden to try to get onto a boat to take them to England. Some of them got away on fishing boats. For several of them it was the second time they had run away from the Nazis. Many more could not secure a place on a ship going to England. With their hopes of escape now gone many committed suicide. Soon the Army and Navy closed the harbor by sinking ships in its entrance and started blowing up the locks and other industrial and military installations that they did not want to fall into German hands intact.

My father continued working in the fishing industry while the Germans still allowed fishing boats access to the North Sea to fish under German surveillance. An aunt of mine, Aunt Lies, worked for a Jewish actress called Claartje who had married a non-Jewish Theater producer called Bob Peters. They lived in Amsterdam. Through her we were kept informed of what was happening to the Jewish population of Amsterdam. My father told aunt Lies that he would like to supply Jewish people in Amsterdam with fish. The job of delivering the fish usually fell on my shoulders, while sometimes my sister Harriet took care of the delivery. I would take the train to Amsterdam and from there I would walk to Bob Peters' house to deliver the fish. Often they would ask me to stay the night, so I got to know some of the people in what I remember as a very large house with many levels and stairwells. There were usually around eight to ten people, including some children, with their luggage always close at hand. Different people came and went all the time.

We never knew what was going to happen or when the Germans would raid the house. I was often given the job of notifying people in times of trouble.

Claartje had a sister who was staying in the house. Her name was Suzanne and I got to know her. One night she was sitting beside me as we were talking. She took the Star of David from her blouse and gave it to me. We were both about 17 years old at the time. I put it in my pocket. The next time that I went to deliver fish I was told Suzanne was no longer there. I was told she had been picked up by the Germans.

After the war I went to see Claartje Peters to find out if Suzanne was still alive. I had the Star that Suzanne had given me with me. Claartje told me that Suzanne had not returned. I did not have the heart to ask her how Suzanne had died. It just did not seem right at the time. I showed her the star that Suzanne had given me and asked her if she wanted it. She said: "You keep it, Art". I learned that Claartje was the only one of her family who had survived the war. I passed the star on to my son Tim, who will in turn pass it on to his daughter Danielle. In that way the lessons from Suzanne's star will stay alive.

We had to wear our sweaters

Anthonia Huysman

My brother and I played outside in Groningen. We were half-Jewish (our father was Jewish) and we had been issued with stars and ordered to wear them. They were sewn onto our sweaters. We did not like sweaters, we would take them off and hide them behind some bushes. I remember my mother yelling and crying for us to put them on. We could not understand why. We all survived the war, though my father did have to go into hiding on a farm for some time.

Betrayed

Wim Bongers

I remember people I had known all my life in my hometown suddenly walking around with a yellow star on their chests with the word 'Jew' (Jood) in dark black letters in its center. Nobody knew that there were so many Jews in Hoorn. We were Roman Catholics, had our animosities with Protestant kids and knew pretty much who they were, but those of the Jewish faith were generally not in the picture.

The first violent round-up of Jews took place in Amsterdam's Jewish district. More than 400 men were sent to Mauthausen Concentration Camp. I remember this very distinctly, because one of these men was the son of a Hoorn jeweler who happened to be visiting a cousin in Amsterdam at that time. He was definitely 'in the wrong place at the wrong time'.

From that time on Jewish people lived in fear. Many removed and discarded their yellow stars and went into hiding wherever a hiding place could be found. Most found places in the homes of helpful citizens, others hid in churches, boats, barns, empty houses, attics, cellars, windmills, whatever was available.

Though my parents had seven children and were far from rich we suddenly had three more people in our household: a Jewish mother named Carla and her two young daughters, Marja and Rodie. The mother was a nurse in an Amsterdam hospital and we found out soon after that she would be away frequently for long periods as she was helping other Jews from Amsterdam find hiding places.

Carla did not look very Jewish. Her husband had already been picked up by the Gestapo and sent to a concentration camp. Marja had the same features as her dad, she looked Jewish with her dark hair, brown eyes and prominent nose. Rodie looked more like her mom, she had light blond hair and blue eyes.

Carla was picked up and questioned by the Gestapo many times, but was always released again. She knew how to talk herself out of dangerous situations. However, as lucky as she was, sometime early in 1944 she again went on a mission which turned out to be her last. She never returned.

When these three Jewish people came to our house certain house rules were changed and some new rules were made. We were told by our parents never to tell our friends or others about the three extra people in our house, not even our best friends. The two Jewish girls were told to remain strictly within the confines of the house and backyard, never to get closer to a window than three feet and never to answer or go near one of the outside doors. When playing in the backyard they were not to yell out loudly nor to laugh or giggle. The backyard was enclosed with a high stone wall, with two big doors that functioned as a gate and were closed with a beam. The doors opened up to a street called Warmoes Street (Warmoesstraat).

One of my mother's sisters, our Aunt Dien, lived In another part of Hoorn. She was married to Uncle John Molenaar. Their home was on Meerens Street (Meerensstraat), where like us they had Jewish people in hiding. First there was one, a little boy of about six years old and then suddenly there were eleven of all ages. An incident with catastrophic results caused the Jews to have to move suddenly to a different place, right next door to us in the Pieterselie Alley (Pieterseliesteeg) in the carpentry shop of John's father, 'Old Molenaar' as he was known to us.

The incident took place on July 7, 1944 when a squadron of Allied bombers flew over our city on its way to Germany. It was about 8.45 in the morning. I remember the sky was black with planes, obscuring the sun. The sound was tremendous, loud and droning. A friend and I were on our way to school, just crossing Church Square (Kerkplein). We were fascinated by what we heard and saw and stood still for a while. The airplanes were flying very high, leaving vapor trails that formed a long white cloud behind them, visible for many miles. Suddenly we saw a flash of light, we heard a loud explosion and saw parts of planes, opened parachutes and unexploded bombs hurtling down. The sirens on top of the church and other buildings were activated and wailed their eerie blaring sound. A man in Church Alley (Kerksteeg) who stood in the doorway of one of the stores beckoned us and shouted: "get off the street!" We turned around and ran back home.

Later we heard that two bombers had touched wings and crashed down. Parts of the planes were scattered all through the city. There were a number of bomb craters. The most severe damage had occurred in Meerens Street and Drieboom Avenue (Drieboomlaan) where several houses had been flattened or severely damaged. One woman was killed in her house on Drieboom Avenue. The crew of both planes counted ten men, so twenty men in total, of whom thirteen died. One managed to escape after landing in a farmer's field. He went 'underground' in the village of Venhuizen staying with a farmer by the name of Commandeur. He joined the Resistance and rode it out until the end of the war.

With all the commotion going on in the city and especially on Meerens Street Aunt Dien got scared and told the hiding Jews that they had to move to Pieterselie Alley, into her father-in-law's carpentry shop. One by one, disguised and camouflaged with lots of clothing she guided them through the streets of Hoorn, using a different route for every one of them.

When Old Molenaar was still active and working he mainly produced coffins on contract for the local undertaker. Since wood was no longer available he and the shop were idle. The back of the shop annexed onto our back yard, separated by a low three foot high wooden fence. The shop had no toilet, no water no electricity, no cooking facilities, no heat. There was nothing. It was a good place to hide, but unlivable. The backyard fence was opened so that they could use our toilet, an old-fashioned outdoor outhouse with a funnel type barrel receiver situated directly behind the house in our backyard. When it came to obtaining water, cooking their meals and washing their clothes our kitchen became their kitchen. Of course they would always ask if it was okay so that they would not interfere with our requirements.

As fall became winter it got very cold in the carpentry shop. We all donated a blanket from our beds to them. They huddled together to keep themselves warm.

Things were not going well at Aunt Dien's on Meerens Street. She was being questioned. My mom had taken the two Jewish girls, Marja and Rodie to the Hairdresser. While they were there they suddenly saw Aunt Dien walking by between two tall men each wearing a raincoat. They both had one hand hidden in one of their coat-pockets. They were walking in the direction of our house. Mom thought for a moment, did not like what she saw and decided not to take the girls back to the house, but instead brought them to the sacristy of our church. In the meantime Aunt Dien and the two men had reached their destination, the rear entrance to our house, the wooden gate on Warmoes Street. It was locked with the beam, but she yelled "It's Aunt Dien," which led someone to remove the beam and give her and the two men access to our backyard. My sister Greta and I were sitting right across from the gate, next to the kitchen door peeling and scraping some potatoes we still had. We looked up and saw guns in the hands of the two men, who shouted: "Hands up, you're all under arrest!"

Greta threw the basket with potatoes aside, grabbed me by the arm and we both ran into the house straight up the stairs to the second floor. There sitting right in the open was our radio, still tuned to the frequency of the BBC. That in itself was sufficient to get arrested and sent to prison. Greta quickly removed her apron and threw it over the radio, I grabbed a pillow and placed in on top of the apron. We both went into a large walk-in clothes closet, closed the door and waited in the dark, shaking with fear. It did not take long until we heard footsteps coming up the stairs and someone milling about. Suddenly the closet door was opened and we heard somebody say: "Come on out." We both emerged. Greta got a kick in the behind, she almost tumbled down the stairs and I was held to identify the ID-cards the man who had come upstairs held in his hands.

I was surprised that he spoke Dutch. He questioned me calmly. "Who is this person?" and "Who is this?" he asked as he showed me the different ID-cards he had collected from the other people in the house. "This is my brother Louis," I said, "and this one I don't know." I identified the family members and for the Jewish people hiding with us I said: "I don't know." We had been told to do it this way, although in reality this identified the Jews. When it came to the ID of my cousin Cor, who was also in the house, we encountered some difficulties. His mother was of Spanish ancestry, she had a dark complexion and so had Cor. When I said that he was my cousin I was shouted down: "No he is a Jew!" I insisted that he was my cousin, the man questioning me insisted that he was Jewish. He put his handgun up to my temple and asked again: "who is this?" I again said: "that's my cousin." He finally believed me. He led me to the stairs and I ran down as fast as I could, with him behind me. The Jews were all lined up in the hallway and kitchen, ready to be led out onto the street. Cousin Cor was begging one of the young mothers to hand him her little girl, about two years old. "No," she said, "if we have to go she will have to go as well."

The Jews were led to the police station on Cheese Market Square (Kaasmarkt). One of the men managed to escape via our backyard. He jumped the fence to the neighbor's backyard and the next fence into the street. After being held in the police station for a short period the Jews were transported in vans out of town, to end up in one of the concentration camps, we don't know where.

While all this was going on my two years older brother Ap had managed to run over to the horse stables where my father was working at the time and warned him not to come home. He stayed away for a few days. We had learned in the meantime that the two men who had come with Aunt Dien were so-called bounty-seekers, traitors. They had no cause to do us any harm, they had been awarded with the standard fees, whatever they got for bringing in a Jew. Of course they missed out on the payment for the one that escaped. For this we were scrutinized and pestered for many weeks afterwards, them thinking that the escapee was still in our midst. But he was long gone, we had no idea where to.

After the war Marja and Rodie, the two Jewish girls reappeared, they had been found by a surviving uncle and the three of them moved to Israel. The Jewish man who had escaped via our backyard came to see us and thank us in the beginning of August of 1945. He had a lot to tell my parents. He knew that the other Jews who had been caught in our house had been killed and cremated in Bergen-Belsen Concentration Camp.

Aunt Dien and Uncle John were no longer welcome in our household, although they managed to get a tree planted in their name somewhere in Israel for their 'bravery'. My parents never received anything. No accolades, no thanks, no recognition. Not that they wanted this, they were not looking for gratitude.

They had disappeared

Olga Chesbrough

When we grew up a Jewish family lived next to us. My brother and I and the Jewish children played together all the time, in their house, in our house. One morning the family had disappeared overnight. Mother could not tell us kids what had happened, or where the family had moved to.

Not allowed to play together

Liesbeth Boysen-van den Blink

During the first months of the war I became friends with a girl named Kitty. She was a year older than I. Together we baby-sat for my aunt and walked her little girl. One day Kitty appeared with a big Star of David on her coat. I did not know anything about Jews. Kitty was a friend just like the others. It didn't take long or Kitty was no longer allowed to go to school! That made me very mad and I couldn't understand why! I decided to bring her homework after school, so that when she came back she wouldn't have missed too much.

Kitty's backyard was like a courtyard with a big high wooden fence and a gate. I had a chance to tell her that I would be by every day and she waited by the gate. We talked and she told me sadly that I couldn't come in. This lasted for a week. Then when I came home Opa (who I was staying with in Den Briel, far away from my parents in Eindhoven) told me that I wasn't allowed to do that anymore, but I did anyway!

Two days later, I received another talk from Opa. He was very upset and told me that two men had come to the house and they had said that if I went on visiting Kitty, they would kill him. Opa said, with lots of sadness: "please, please stop".

The next day coming home from school with some friends, we came by the alley where Kitty lived. On the corner of the alley stood a man dressed totally in black. Our group of girls commented on this strange sight. Then we saw another man at the end of the alley dressed the same. Now that was scary. Kitty's gate was closed, so I didn't stop. At night I told Opa about these strange men. Opa said: "remember I told you about the bad men that came to the house, those are the men watching you. Please, please be careful." I talked some of my friends into walking home via a different route. They were scared. I had nightmares about these men for a long time. At the end of that summer we moved back to Eindhoven.

I never saw my friend Kitty again. This memory stayed with me until this day. About ten years ago we heard about a list to trace missing persons and we found the family listed. Mrs. Katan, Kitty and her two brothers died in Auschwitz in 1942. Mr. Katan in 1943.

They wanted to take me

Jerry Meents

My father, Hartog Meents was Jewish, my mother, Louisa Volger was not. Eight children were born to this couple, who had a mixed marriage in Nazi terms. Three children were born before the start of the war in 1940, four during the occupation and one after Holland was liberated. We lived in a part of South Amsterdam that was predominantly Jewish.

Early in the war fighting broke out between Jewish youth groups and a Dutch paramilitary group of Nazi collaborators. One of the collaborators was killed. The Germans closed off the old Jewish section of Amsterdam with barbed wire and guarded the entrances. After the wire came down, we could visit our relatives again, who lived in the area.

After some more scuffles in which the collaborators had to run for their lives the Germans rounded up more than 400 Jewish men and sent them to Mauthausen Concentration Camp. One of the men lived next door to us. Two months after he had been deported our neighbor got a notice from Mauthausen that her son was dead. I can still hear this lady scream in pain and helplessness. She could be heard a block away.

Just before my tenth birthday all Jewish children had to leave the public schools and were allowed in Jewish schools only. Now there was a problem. According to the Germans I was a half-Jew, which meant I was supposed to stay in the public school. But because all my friends were Jewish and because I had grown up around Jewish kids I joined them in the Jewish school in the Transvaal neighborhood of Amsterdam. When the Germans decreed that all Jews had to wear a yellow Star of David on their clothes there was some confusion about who was exactly considered Jewish, so I wore the star for about three months. When my mother found out that I did not have to wear it, she took it off my clothes.

My father and others in his situation had to be registered as being married to a non-Jew.

In October of 1942 there was a big round-up in our neighborhood during which the Germans took my best friend and his family away.

Rumors held that the Jewish people were being sent to Sobibor in Poland to work. No one knew that Sobibor was an extermination camp.

In May of 1943 the last big round-up took place in the old Jewish neighborhood. In this round-up the Germans took my grandfather and his wife and an aunt with her husband and two children. My aunt had already lost a 17-year old son who perished in Auschwitz a year earlier. An uncle had also already lost a son in Auschwitz.

About one month later most of the remaining Jews were picked up in East and South Amsterdam. During this raid a German and a Dutch policeman came to our apartment to see if there were any Jews. My father was hiding behind the living room door and was not discovered. The Dutch collaborator looked at me and said: "He is a Jew," and wanted to take me, all because I had black hair and brown eyes. But because a little brother had been born just before the round-up my mother's parents were visiting. My grandfather ignored the Dutch policeman and spoke to the German one and they left without me.

Jewish men who were married to a non-Jew had to report for work camps. My father was sent to a camp called Vledder. With no money coming in and six children, my mother started to clean apartments and I had to clean our own house, look after the other kids, and cook. Thirteen weeks later my father came home on leave for a week and a few days later he had to turn in his papers from the camp and he did not have to return to Vledder. I know that my mother talked to her priest, our family physician and whomever more. I don't know who had the influence or what they said, but my father could stay home.

My grandfather, Gerrit Meents, was 70 years old when he was murdered in Sobibor. In fact, 90% of my friends from the street I lived on were murdered in this extermination camp or in Auschwitz. One day I still played with them. The next day they were gone, never to be seen again. I had a girlfriend, my first great love, who lived across the street. She was taken away with her family and murdered in Sobibor.

Their train went east

Truus Leader

My father took us one Sunday to go see our mother at the hospital in Castricum, about 25 miles from Amsterdam. We were very happy because we had to take the train. We went to Central Station and I watched as many people were standing around while German soldiers seemed to guard them. Men, women and children with yellow stars on their coats. A freight train stopped and the doors were opened. The people under guard were ordered to get in. I watched a girl my age with a beautiful doll. I never had my own doll and envied her. She also got on the train with the other people. I asked my father why they had to go on a train without windows? He replied: "Don't look at them." We got on our nice train with leather seats. I watched as the freight train was leaving the station. It went east, our train went west.

Betrayed II

Jan de Zwager

I
n May of 1940 I had just turned eight, my brother Kees would turn seven in June. Father was 37, Mother 32 and after Kees came Nico (6), Mia (4), Hannie (3), Rob (almost 2) and Elsje was on the way. A bit much maybe... we wondered some time later. But upon the suggestion that it should be enough my mother would answer: "tell that to your father." Knowing Father that never happened.

We lived in Haarlem and got through the first years of the war well enough, with another baby every fifteen months or so. Mother had a help, a young girl called Gerda, she was two or three years older than us. One day something happened that we did not understand. Father, Mother and Gerda were hauled off by the Germans in a police van. We stayed behind wondering what was going on. I stayed home with the little ones. Kees told the authorities at school that I could not come, he gave no explanation, we did not know anything.

Three or four days later I put on my roller skates and went to Aunt Toos in Heemstede, about five miles away. She had the fright of her life. She knew of course that my sudden appearance could bode nothing but bad news. So she got on her bike and went to our house, with me in tow on my roller skates.

Mother had been locked up in Smede Street, Father had been transported to the large prison on Wetering Sconce (Weteringschans), a street in central Amsterdam. After a week Mother came home. She told us that Gerda was

Jewish. It was absolutely forbidden to have a Jewish person live and work in a non-Jewish household.

Father worked for the Arbeiderspers, a newspaper and book publishing company which was aligned to the labor movement before the war, but had been put under Nazi leadership at the start of the occupation. Many of the employees were active in the Resistance, helping out Jewish children like Gerda. My father's boss, Mr. Noordhof, was the liaison in this matter. He came to Haarlem once a week to bring food and pass on information about Father. Also once each week Mother, Kees and I would go to the prison, drop off special vitamin drinks with forbidden chunks of butter in them. We dropped them off at a counter in the prison and also clothes and shoes in packages for Father.

Towards the corner of the building in one of the cells at the top right was where Father was supposed to be. Mr. Noordhof would have informed him of the appointed time of our weekly visits. "Father!... Father!... Faaather..." Kees and I shouted and his arm would appear through the bars and wave to us.

After two months he was transferred to Vught Concentration Camp. From that time on his boss could not bring us much more news. Mother said: "Go to mass every morning, go to communion and pray. Especially to Holy Mary. Because if you do that, I am sure he will be home before Christmas." We prayed and prayed and prayed, on our knees, also in the evening at home.

Mr. Noordhof suddenly had news for us again in November. Would Mary be able to pull it off, Father home before Christmas? On the 22nd, or maybe the 23rd of December 1944 Mr. Noordhof came by again. It was in the evening. "I have good news for you," he said. "Your father is one of a first group that is being released, maybe even soon." The doorbell rang. Mother opened the door, with us close behind her... There he was, bald, skinny, gunny sack on his back with his belongings. Mr. Noordhof had planned it so that there was a little time between the news and Father's arrival to get us into a special mood. Party, of course! We sang Father's favorite songs and then to bed. It was late.

Father and Mother had been betrayed by someone, which happened often in those days. Who could have done such a thing? A Mrs. Van L. often visited for coffee. She liked to talk. Did she know? Mother did not remember, many years later, when we discussed it. But still... Mrs. Van L.'s pretty young daughter was deeply in love with a German officer... so maybe? One thing was sure, Mrs. Van L. did not come over for coffee any more, did she know about the suffering...? So maybe...?

We asked Father how life was in his cell and in Vught: no answer. He only said the he and three other men in his cell did gymnastics for hours on end to keep in shape. The only story we heard about Vught came from one of Father's fellow prisoners there. He told Mother the following: Early in the morning a prisoner who had tried to escape during the night was violently beaten in front of the assembled prisoners during roll-call. Father could not bear to watch this and was prepared to jump out of the orderly formation until a friend said to him: "Nico, think of your wife and kids. Close your eyes..."

Poor Gerda... we received her very last news from a couple from Amsterdam who were being transported to Germany in the same carriage as she was. At night at some railway station a few people had a chance to escape, including this couple. They said: "Come on Gerda..." She said: "No! I have already caused great grief for one large family, I'll stay and see what happens..."

Hiding from the Nazis

Jaap Matz

I was ten years old when the German army invaded Holland. My brother Bernard was twelve and our sister Bonja was five. We lived in Scheveningen, where we were born.

In August of 1942 a good friend of my parents came to visit. He was a member of the Resistance. He pointed out to my parents that, like elsewhere, Jewish families were being picked up in Scheveningen. He said that he had a temporary hiding place for my brother Bernard and me. And that's how the most miserable episode in my life began, which ended a year later when we entered the farmhouse of the Van Vliet Family.

For a year we tramped around in The Hague, Delft and Baarn. Sometimes we were together, sometimes on our own, sometimes in one spot for two or three weeks, occasionally for a month. Most people were afraid of the Nazis and not without reason. If someone was suspected of harboring people hiding from the authorities, they would be treated atrociously in prison. Infamous was the prison in Scheveningen that was called the 'Orange Hotel'. Poor people without morals became traitors for money. The enemy was extremely cruel.

In August of 1943 someone from the Resistance brought us to the farm of the Van Vliets in Schipluiden. We walked there from Delft. The driveway flanked by willow trees and the beautiful linden tree in front of the house impressed us greatly. Piet van Vliet welcomed

41

us, he was a fatherly person, who had taken over management of the farm after his parents had died. During the twenty months until liberation we interacted mostly with Toos. She was a little older than Bernard and was always in a cheerful mood. We also got on very well with Wim. Cor was a quiet boy and a hard worker. Geer was learning the horticultural trade. Arie was in hiding from the Germans and Riet and Toos did housekeeping inside the farmhouse with the assistance of their cousin Corry Vieveen.

During the day we took turns to stand guard. If someone came up the driveway between the willows we told one of the girls. If it was a visiting relative we would go into our hiding place. In the room adjacent to the living room were two 'closet beds'. Between the two beds was a deep closet with suits, dresses and coats, There were shoes on the floor. Between the wall and the clothes were two low benches. We sat there safely for hours while the family was chatting away with their company. At night we slept behind the dog kennel in the haystack.

The Germans shot rockets at England from the coastal area. One of the places they were launched from was Delft. The rockets flew across the fields between us and the neighboring farm. That was very noisy.

Although it was strictly forbidden, the boys listened to the BBC's Dutch language service from London every night at eight. They had hidden a radio in a bale of straw. There was a small, obscured opening to reach its controls. We knew by now that the enemy was losing the war and that it would not take long before we would be liberated.

Almost every night during the final years of the

occupation we heard a droning in the sky: hundreds upon hundreds of English and American bombers on their way to Germany, where they were going to bomb factories and cities. I have always wondered why a few of those planes did not destroy the railway lines to the death camps: six million Jews and a half million Gypsies were transported to these camps by train, only a handful of them survived. I never heard a satisfactory answer

It was the last winter of the war. The canal behind the haystack had frozen over, it was very cold. Just like every night, one of the boys brought us to the haystack and took the dog out of its kennel. We climbed into the kennel, pushed the back panel away, crawled into our hiding place and closed the trap door. Good night farm! In the middle of the night we suddenly woke up, startled: the dog was barking so loudly that it frightened us. To our great dismay we heard voices speaking German and boots stamping around in the snow. Horses belonging to the Germans were eating the scant remainder of the hay that still covered our hiding place.

The loud barking woke Wim up. He ran to the door grabbing a warm overcoat on the way. He opened the door and saw the German soldiers and the horses. He knew that he and the two Jewish boys were in mortal danger. Fortunately he kept his wits about him. He shouted in German: "Come in, I have beer for you." The bottles of beer that Wim gave to the Germans were being saved for Liberation Day. One of the boys took us out of our hiding place and smuggled us into the house, to the deep closet. We stayed in there all day. In the early evening the door to the room opened and the German sergeant came in. He was looking for a bed. Fortunately someone who had noticed him fetched Wim, who gave the German a bed in one of the upstairs bedrooms. When all the Germans were asleep, we were taken to the attic above the cow barn. There were some bales of straw. Some of these were shoved aside, creating a small open space. We spent fourteen days there. We could hear the soldiers. They had moved into the barn below us and slept on the straw. There was snow on the roof tiles. It was very cold.

Piet who visited us regularly realized that this could not continue. He put his best suit on and went to the local priest and told him that a band of German deserters had moved into the farm uninvited. He also told them that he was hiding Jews. The priest set Piet's mind at rest: "Don't worry, everything will be fine!"

That same day the deserters and their horses were taken away by the German police, the dreaded Gestapo. The boys carried us downstairs. Gradually our health, which had suffered severely from our isolation in the cold attic, improved.

Thanks to the hidden radio we knew that we would be liberated soon. Schipluiden and the surrounding area were liberated by French-speaking Canadians. A spontaneous party took place in the village that night. Because Bernard and I did not know what had become of our parents and our sister we did not feel like celebrating, unfortunately. While the crowd jeered and cheered, the hair of some young 'ladies' who had had inappropriate relations with German soldiers was cut off.

After several days a good friend of our parents, Mrs. Maso, came to get us. She had been very active in the Resistance. Piet said to us: "I have set aside the money

I received every month for your keep". He gave us the bankbook.

Soon lists were published with the names of Jews who had been murdered in the extermination camps. We then realized that we had no parents and no sister anymore. In addition to uncles, aunts and cousins who were no longer alive, we heard that my mother's brother, who lived in the Dutch East Indies with his family, had perished in a Japanese concentration camp.

Several months later it was a complete surprise when our aunt Marie returned from Bergen-Belsen. Once she had regained her strength she adopted us. Bernard went to Israel in 1951 and I followed in 1952. We have always stayed in close contact with the De Vries family. The family has received the award from 'Yad Vashem' that is given to heroes who have endangered their own lives to save persecuted Jews.

He held no grudge

Rita Binder

A Jewish man lived in hiding in our home for over a year, which was kept secret from us children. When he heard of a forthcoming round-up he disappeared, returning when all was safe. His wife and children perished in a concentration camp. Yet he held no grudge. Of course we heard of his story and others after the war. I have a letter from our Jewish friend in which he stated: "The war is over."

After the Germans were driven out my father offered him help so he could get back in business. His reply was: "Although I have only 25 cents now I will make it." And he did. He remarried, worked very hard and became a millionaire. He showed his gratitude to my father by having 90 trees planted in Israel on his birthday.

Although the Germans were our enemies I am with our Jewish friend who held no grudge. He remained close friends with our family in Holland and with us until his death in 2007 at 91 years.

Hiding Jewish friends

Hetty Wear

My father had a career in the Dutch army, and as a result we lived in several cities during the 1930s. In 1938 we ended up in Gorinchem.

A day or so after we arrived my mother went to do some shopping. She went into a store to buy some soap. As soon as she saw the lady behind the counter she was sure she knew her. "Are you Esther?" Mother asked. When the lady answered "yes, I am," my mom asked her if she could guess who she was in turn. It did not take long. As my mother told us later she called out: "Is it really you Greta?" Esther hurried from behind the counter and hugged my mother and called her husband to look after the store, so my mother could come in for tea. My mother knew Esther because at one time, before she was married, she had worked for Esther's father who owned a small department store in Bergen op Zoom. Esther was a young girl then, only eleven years old. They had lost touch over the years. We moved a lot and Mom had no relatives in Bergen op Zoom any more. Now the friendship was renewed.

Esther and her husband Sam were Jewish. They were in their early thirties and worked hard in their store. It was not long before my parents and I met the rest of Sam's family. His parents lived nearby and so did his younger sister with her husband. They lived in a large house, where the parents lived downstairs and his sister with her husband, newly-weds, had the second floor.

47

Housing was hard to get and this was the reason they lived together.

These were actually the first people my parents got to know in Gorinchem, save for some of Dad's colleagues. Soon after we moved, the army was mobilized and conscripts and reserves were called up. I remember how the streets were full of soldiers. It seemed as if anyone who had ever been in uniform was there. Sam too was in uniform, leaving Esther to tend the store. My dad was a sergeant-major. He was not with a fighting force, but was with what we called the Red Cross. He had a small red cross on both sides of the collar of his uniform and often wore a white band with a red cross around his arm. It was his job among other things to teach first aid to the soldiers.

On May 10, 1939 Dad celebrated 25 years of service. Little did we know that exactly a year later we would be at war. When that happened just the two of us, my mother and I, were together as I was an only child. We woke that morning very early, the roar of many planes woke us up. We opened the window in my parents' bedroom to look out. We saw many people standing in the street, everyone looking up and wondering what this was. Were these German planes? We did not know until someone went back inside his house and turned on the radio. He came back out shouting that we were being invaded by Germany. I still remember how I got sick to my stomach, and I had not even had breakfast yet. I did not go to school that day. Like everyone else we waited to see what would happen next.

It was another month before we heard from my dad. One day when I came home, Mom told me Dad was okay. Dad had wired some money. Mother said that was his way of telling us he was fine. Still it took until the end of summer before my father was sent home on 70% of his salary.

The two following years were much the same as in the rest of the country. Food was rationed and everyone was forced to carry an ID card. This card had your picture on it as well as your fingerprint. If you were Jewish it had a large letter J on it as well. Sam and Esther's store had a big sign over the entrance that read 'Jewish Business', which was intended to stop Germans from buying there.

In 1941 a big event happened in our family. After all these years my parents had another baby and I finally had a baby sister. The rations my mother received for the new baby included six diapers. Friends and family helped out with baby-clothes and such things. Mom and I went and chose a nice baby carriage. It was one thing the Germans had not yet gotten around to hauling off to Germany.

In 1942 things got bad for the Jewish people. One day in school the principal came in with a couple of Germans. I think they were SS officers. The names of three of our students were called out. All three were Jewish. They were told to go with the officers. We were all stunned. Our teacher went with them, leaving us behind. Someone started to sing the Dutch national anthem. Everyone joined in. The principal rushed back in. "Stop. Stop," he yelled, "we will all get into trouble". He was right. The SS insisted we all be called in and questioned. One by one we went into the office and as it turned out we were all asked the same question: who started the singing? My answer was that I did not know, it was someone behind me, so I had no way of knowing who it was. All of us had a similar answer.

I was upset when I got home and told my parents how three students had been taken away. The three of us sat around the table and Dad told me how he and my mom had plans to help Esther and Sam. I understood that I must not tell anyone. My mom had already spoken to Esther, who said that she did not want to go into hiding because "she had not done anything." My dad explained over and over that although that was true, the Germans would take them away to a concentration camp regardless. Finally she agreed, and the planning began.

At the end of August they would put a sign on their door that said they were closed for two weeks of vacation. This was not unusual in Holland. They would then walk over to our place and not go home again. I remember saying that everyone knew we were friends and that it would be likely the Germans would come to our house to look for them. My dad explained that he had found a very good hiding place for them, a little way out of town. But we could not take them there until it got dark earlier in the evening, perhaps October. Esther had trouble leaving everything behind. Although Dad said it was only 'stuff', my mom understood that certain things are special. There was the bone china and silver cutlery she had inherited from her mother, who had died young. And so it happened that my mother went to the store every day with my sister in the baby carriage. There in the room behind the store they would load the things in the carriage under the mattress. First the china bit by bit, after that the silver, followed by their clothes and shoes and last some of the stock that they had in the store. My little sister always sat much higher in the carriage when they came home than when they had left.

I helped my mom get the things out of the carriage and take them to the attic where we packed them in boxes. We had boxes of soap, lipstick and other make-up. At that time we still thought the war would not last that long and that this was stock to go back into the business for them. So the summer went by and true to plan they locked the door one day in the last week of August and walked over to our house.

We had decided that they would sleep in the spare bedroom on the third floor attic. You had to get there through a trapdoor in the floor. Dad said if the worst happened to drag something heavy over the trapdoor, so that it would be impossible to open it. If there were ever any questions we would say that it was stuck and we had never used the attic. They were vague plans at best. Although there was a window in the spare bedroom, it was in the roof. You could push it open, but I doubt if Sam and Esther could have climbed out of it. During the day they stayed upstairs, in the evenings they were downstairs with us. The only other person who knew about them was Jenny. Jenny came Mondays to Fridays from eight until two to help with the housework. She had to be told and was given the choice to quit if she was too afraid. Jenny chose to stay, and never told anyone.

I walked by the store every day, and on the 16th day after Esther and Sam had left the Germans broke in. Soon after some officers were living in the upstairs living-quarters. When people began asking me if I knew where Esther and Sam had gone, I said that I had heard that they had plans to go to Switzerland, but I could not be sure if they had made it.

The place Dad had picked for them was about four

miles out of town, near a place called Arkel. The house was near what I believe was a pumping-station and the man living in the house was in charge of it. The house sat all by itself, you could look out over a long distance and the land being flat no one could come near without being seen even at quite a distance. It certainly was a safe place. October came and a day was set for the move. We even took note of the phase of the moon, because it had to be as dark as possible. The baby-carriage was packed once again with belongings, mostly clothes. The plan was that I would stay with my sister and Mom and Dad would walk them to their hiding place. I could see that my mother was very nervous. Suddenly I had a better idea. "Let me go, you stay with Anneke" I said to my mother. "I can't let you do that my dear child", she said. "I am not a child, I am 18 years old," I replied. This went back and forth for a while, but we settled it. Esther would push the carriage with Dad walking beside it. I would walk with Sam, keeping our distance from them, so we would look like two different couples. Dad said the tricky part would be 'Villa Argo'. This villa was halfway between Gorinchem and Arkel, and had been the home of our city's mayor. The Germans had requisitioned it and turned it into an officers' club. We had to go past it, there was no other way.

We started out. With the blackout in force and a dark moon it was indeed a pitch black night. Dad and Esther led the way. Sam and I walked a good sixty feet behind them as planned. Dad and I also wheeled our bicycles beside us, because we had to get back before ten. That was the curfew at that time. Soon we came to Villa Argo. I could make out Germans standing outside, because they were smoking and I could see the light of their cigarettes in the dark. They called out 'Good Evening' in German. Normally we would not have given them the time of day, but we did not want any of them to come over, if only to pick on us, so Dad replied 'Evening' and when our turn came to walk by them I did the same. We got to the house safely and Dad and I cycled home. We felt greatly relieved.

Meanwhile Sam's sister Della and her husband Bert asked if they could put some stuff in our attic, some boxes of food, and I believe some clothes. Dad urged them to go into hiding and they said they were working on it and planned to leave their home soon. One evening in late October the doorbell rang. We looked at each other. It was past curfew, who could this be? Puzzled both my parents went to the door. There stood Della and Bert. They whispered: "Can we come in?" Della seemed to be in shock, Bert was trying to calm her. Mother made coffee, not knowing what else to do. Gradually the story came out. They had all been asleep, but at 5 a.m. they had heard a loud noise like car doors being slammed. Looking out the upstairs windows they saw the Germans coming to their front door. They knew their parents did not have a chance to get away, but they suddenly decided to try and hide. In their room there was a window that led onto the roof. Quickly they made the bed and crawled out the window and inched their way to the neighbor's house. The two houses were alike and were under one roof. They made it to the window in the neighbor's roof. The window was slightly open as there was some laundry hanging upstairs and people often let a little air in to help dry the clothes.

All day long they sat in that attic, not making a sound.

Finally when it was dark they ventured downstairs, surprising their neighbors and they explained how they had hidden in the attic. Their neighbors were kind enough, made tea for them and something to eat. They told them what had happened to Della's parents. The noise outside had woken them up too. They had gone to the door and saw the Germans and the waiting van to transport the captured Jews. It was one of those vans with doors in the back. The couple had been brought out of the house and at that point the neighbor asked if she could not let them come in first and have some breakfast. Could she at least make some coffee for these people? The German made some rude remark about them being Jews, not regular people, and no, there would be no stopping for coffee. While this little distraction took place, Sam's father took his wife by the hand and ran to the bridge that was just at the left of their house. This bridge spanned a canal, at a point very close to where it connected with the Merwede river, a wide tributary of the Rhine. Together they jumped into the canal, preferring to die rather than go with the Gestapo. Alas, it made things worse. There was a rowboat moored nearby, and the Germans simply used it to haul the unfortunate people into the boat and put them, wet as they were, into the van. The neighbors also told Della and Bert that the Germans had inquired who else lived next door and that they had told them no one else as far as they knew. However, kind as they were the neighbors insisted Della and Bert could not stay, because they were too afraid. So Della and Bert left and headed for our house.

In case the Germans were still searching for them, Dad found a quick temporary hiding place. It was a cellar and you could enter it from the street by going down some stairs on the outside. It was a miserable place to be. Every evening Dad brought them food and a thermos of coffee. When it looked like there was no ongoing search for them they came back to our house. Once again the spare bed in the attic was occupied.

Della and Bert lived with us for several weeks, until a more permanent place was found for them, a boarding house run by a widow. There were some people there from other parts of the country who had lost their homes through bombing and other war damage. She even had a German billeted there. It was decided that Bert would move through the house freely, Della would stay in their room. She would be 'sick'.The landlady thought she looked too Jewish with her dark hair and eyes.

Not long after all this happened my Dad was arrested. One morning we were still having breakfast when there was a loud banging on the door and in walked two SS-men and a Dutch guy, a collaborator. "Come with us," they ordered. Dad, always the cool one, said that he would finish his breakfast first. "No, you won't," said the Dutch guy, and yanked him roughly by his shirt-sleeve tearing the shirt. I ran to my dad protesting that he had done nothing, but they took him away anyway, all the way to Rotterdam. There was a big jail there full of political prisoners we heard later. Along with my dad a teacher from the local high school was taken away as well as our neighbor across the street, who ran a tobacco store and lived behind and above his store. This man had five children and we felt so bad for his wife.

The teacher and my dad knew each other well. Sometimes they would go sailing together. Mr. V.

taught physics and chemistry in the highest class of the local high school. I know now that they were in the Resistance together, at the time I did not know that. For eight days we heard nothing about my father, we were not even sure where he was. After eight sleepless nights and lots of worrying on our part my dad was suddenly back. He had not shaved all those days and looked a mess. We were overjoyed. Out of nowhere flowers were delivered to our house, I guess the news spread quickly.

Dad told us he spent most of the time in his cell. Three times they had come with papers for him to sign, telling him that would entitle him to get clothes from home and his shaving brush and such. Each time my dad refused to sign, saying he did not need to shave. On the last day he was brought before a high-ranking German officer, who seemed to act as the judge. He asked Dad: "Do you know why you are here?" After Dad replied "No, I do not" the officer said: "Well, you are accused of helping Jews. What is your answer?" It was a good thing that they had someone on hand to translate the questions, it gave Dad more time to think. He had his answer ready: "Would you know of any Jews that would be willing to help me?" At that the officer laughed. To Dad's great surprise he was let go, with a warning, but he was free. Leaving the prison he met his friend the teacher, also set free. Our neighbor who had been the third man taken that day was shot dead. It had been a close call for Dad and Mr. V.

In 1943 we found out that things were not good with Esther and Sam. The people that had seemed so nice charged them an outrageous price for staying in the house. Although they had known this beforehand, as the war dragged on they were afraid to run out of money. Esther begged my dad to go to Bergen op Zoom and find her father and ask him for more money. Dad went and located her father and came back with an envelope full of money. This was not their only trouble. They got very little food. At 9.30 in the evening their host would start to yawn and remark that it was 'time' again. That meant they had to go to bed. Once upstairs in the attic, they would smell food being cooked. At various times they would smell ham and eggs, sometimes other foods. It made them even more hungry. Esther sometimes would steal an apple from the pile that was stored in the attic. She would eat the core and stem too, afraid to leave any garbage behind. We decided to bring them back. The host family was told that we wanted to give them a break, and that Sam and Esther would be back.

Although it was not easy feeding two extra people who had no rations, somehow we managed. Dad had gotten a job with the coal bureau. That meant he had to travel by bicycle throughout the Alblasserwaard and had to measure certain buildings that had asked for extra coal for heating. Some of those included farms, even some barges where families lived on board. Often Dad came home with some milk, a piece of cheese, some potatoes all given to him for being as generous as he could with his 'measurements'. Also if he spotted someone fishing he always stopped and bought some fish. In the evenings Esther and I grated sugar beets to make syrup. It was something to put on the awful bread we got. We lived mostly in the kitchen, where we had the warmth of the stove, which was used for heating and cooking.

We had a few close calls, but three times we went through the eye of the needle.

The first time Mom was alone with Sam and Esther upstairs. I had found a job by now and Dad was also at work. There was knocking on the door and the doorbell rang repeatedly. My mother opened the bedroom window, looked down and saw two Germans standing there. She called down asking what they wanted. The answer was: "we need to search your house!" So my mother called back, saying she would come down and let them in. She quickly put Sam and Esther in my bedroom closet. The door was flush with the wall papered in the same color. Mom locked them in and put the large key that served as a handle in the pocket of her apron. She went downstairs and let the Germans in. It seemed they were looking for beds. When they reached my bedroom one German tried to open my closet and they wanted to know what was in there. My mother told them that this was her daughter's closet and that she had the key and was at work. Did they want her to walk over there and get the key? The German waved his hand, it was not important to him. He was interested in the bed on the third floor. Mother told him it was the maid's bed. The German suggested that the daughter should sleep with the maid, so that they could have the room. "Absolutely not!"said my mom. Finally they left.

The second time was an even closer call. It was afternoon and Jenny had already gone home. Again there was the doorbell ringing and the loud knocking. We had a pantry in the kitchen that was built under the stairway, so it was shaped like a triangle. In the narrowest part was a bin for potatoes, however the corner was mostly empty now. Sam quickly crawled in that narrow space just behind the plank that was there to keep the potatoes from rolling out. Esther grabbed a pail, put some water in it and took the dish rag and went on her knees pretending to scrub the floor. The German practically stepped over her. I still don't know what they were looking for.

The third time again was a close call. We had a little Jewish boy living with us. He was just a year and a half old, he was the son of a rabbi. Someone told us they were searching houses throughout the city and they would start in our street soon. This time my mom walked as fast as she could to our doctor. She told him that she could not have them search right now. Our doctor, bless his heart, got a poster-sized piece of white cardboard and printed on it: 'Scarlet Fever. Do not enter! Contagious'. This message was printed in Dutch and German and we put it on the front door. That day they passed our house right by. My mother was so thrilled she kept the sign up for another ten days.

The winter of 1944, known as the Hunger Winter in Holland, was a time to never forget. We were of course in a much better position than the big cities. The farmers around Gorinchem were very good. Of course some people had things to trade. That was not the case for us. Dad was a soldier, we did not have goods to trade. We had the soap from Esther and Sam's store, but we did not dare use that for trading in case someone would put two and two together. Mother sometimes joked that we might not always be fed, but we were certainly clean! After the railway workers went on strike, things got really bad. The Germans said that they would no longer ship any food or goods to the western provinces. Fuel was especially hard to get. Gorinchem is a land of dikes, water and farm land. There are no wooded areas to get some extra firewood. I heard that some people had turned in their armoires to have a coffin made when a loved one died. There simply was no wood. In the winter we took Sam and Esther back to Arkel. We did not have enough food to feed them.

After the war I understood the friendship between Mr. V. and my father. Mr. V. had access to certain materials for teaching his classes. Some of those mixed with other elements could be used to make explosives. Both men had been in the Resistance and had sabotaged the actions of the Germans whenever they could. After the war my dad received a medal at City Hall.

Both couples, Sam and Esther and Della and Bert survived the war. I married a Canadian soldier and moved to Edmonton, Alberta. Sam and Esther followed us there, where they eventually started a store again. Della and Bert also came to Canada.

The little rabbi's son went back to his mother and they hid out together in Giessendam and also survived.

Sam and Della's parents perished in the Holocaust.

The horrors of Camp Vught

Sjenta Wilkinson

When I was 19 years old, in 1942, I became a member of the Resistance, without really being aware of it. I delivered packages for my older brother, who was in hiding. Often I did not know that the packages contained underground newspapers, false passports and other illegal materials. Our house was raided on December 7, 1943 and that was the end of my freedom.

I was interrogated by the SS for an hour, with bright lights shining in my eyes. I was accused of having derailed troop transport trains. Eventually I was put on a train myself and sent to KZ Herzogenbusch, better know as Concentration Camp Vught.

When I look back upon the time 1 spent in there, it makes me shiver. Sometimes it seemed that my life in Vught was not real, but it was real. The SS-men came round every day to taunt the women whose husbands had been shot the day before. You can understand how we women prisoners felt. The grief and anger in some women's minds was uncontrollable.

There was a big room in the camp where they held Jewish children, who just sat there, huddled together. There were no adults, just an older brother or sister of one of the kids, who took care of them all with so much love and attention. We women-prisoners could see them through the window and we smiled at them. We threw them kisses and let them know we loved them.

Sometimes, the door to the room was left open and we would storm in and just let them know that they were precious. However, if we got caught, the punishment was severe. One day a young woman, 17 years old, and I, picked up some sandwiches from the Red Cross with the idea to take them to the children. But we were caught and were punished by having to shovel coal into large containers for the stoves in the barracks. The children were eventually all sent east, where they were murdered upon arrival.

One day the alarms went off for a very long time and all the women had to come forward. We were told that prisoners in barracks 2 had cut off the hair of a prisoner who had been identified as a German spy. This spy prisoner had tried to escape over the electric wire and was shot. All the women from that barracks had to march to the tiny punishment bunker and were locked in there. We heard crying and singing but we were not aware of what was really happening until later. It turned out that ten women had died that night, not being able to breathe. The rest came out in a terrible condition and because of the oxygen deprivation some would never be able to lead a normal life again.

As soon as it was known that this had happened the Political prisoners, of which I was one, were marched without any belongings onto a bus, because the Germans feared reprisals from us. We were shouted at and pushed. Then the SS soldiers with dogs came in and we were told that we would be going somewhere where nobody knew that we existed. Thirteen of us, all women, looked at each other and Han Stokking, a minister's daughter from Amsterdam prayed for us and we promised each other to stick together and have the courage to face anything that would come our way.

We arrived at a factory with blacked out windows. When we were inside the factory, they made it clear to us that if we caused any trouble, there were huge kettles to get rid of us. In other words, we would get murdered.

Then we were introduced to our fellow prisoners, about a hundred in number and we asked why they were there. They were all prostitutes from Amsterdam and Rotterdam who had infected soldiers with syphilis and other sexually transmitted infections. They were injected twice a week with mercury by the prison doctor.

In the factory we had to produce gas masks. We were put to work ten prostitutes with one political prisoner. During this period I was called up to the office and there was a man in plain clothes, a Nazi lawyer and he told me that my boyfriend had approached him to free me and he would try to do that if possible. I cried and he gave me chocolates. I was not supposed to tell anybody and I did not. There was hope for survival again.

On a certain day about 25 of the prostitutes were sent home, back to Amsterdam, cured. I was sent with them, but l was told I was going to another destination. It was scary not knowing what the next step was, but the knowledge that there was a lawyer involved was comforting. I was sent to a prison in Utrecht and was told that l would be taken to court there.

I was in that prison for a month and lost my voice from anxiety. Ineke Staal, a young girl, who had been picked up instead of her father, a police commissioner, saw me and noticed that I could not speak and she shook me and told me to smarten up: "we have to win the war," she said. She was a remarkable girl and after a couple of days l could speak again. Every day we 'played court' to prepare me for my appearance and on a certain day she was taken away and when she came back to the cell, she cried and told me she could go home.

I promised her that I too would fight for my life. A week later l was freed.

The war will never be over

Ruth Gabriele Sarah Silten

My name is Ruth Gabriele Silten. That is the name given me at birth. In 1990 I added another name so that I now am Ruth Gabriele Sarah Silten. Let me just say that I added my name Sarah in time for my Bat Mitzvah (usually celebrated at age 13, but in my case at age 57) which seven of us child survivors chose to celebrate together.

I am a child survivor of the Holocaust or Shoah. That is, I was a child when the war started and still a child when it ended. I was born in Berlin, Germany, to a Jewish family in 1933, a few months after Hitler came to power. My parents decided to seek a safe haven and we emigrated from Germany to Holland in 1938, thinking that Holland was a neutral country. It had maintained neutrality in the First World War and my parents hoped, as did many other people, that it would also remain neutral this time around. We left behind all our other family: my grandparents, aunts, uncles, cousins and so on. All those who stayed in Germany, and that was the majority of them, were murdered in the Shoah. We also left behind all our money, the family's possessions, my toys, our life, language, culture and familiar surroundings. We left behind everything we had ever known.

After the invasion of the Netherlands we were ruled by the Germans, who took over the government and ruled as absolute masters. Before too long, all sorts of repressive rules became law. These laws were promulgated over a period of time, not all at once. That made it easier for the Dutch, Jewish and non-Jewish alike, to accept them, as the Germans well knew. These rules were generally published in a Jewish newspaper, Het Joodsche Weekblad (The Jewish Weekly News). I don't remember them in the order in which they were published, but one of them was that all Jews six years old and over had to wear what we then called the 'Jewish Star', a Magen David, a yellow six-pointed star with black edges and the word 'Jew' in the center. I was seven years old when this happened.

Like all Jewish children I was excluded from regular school. I had to go to a Jewish school which was not a day school or religious school as we now know it, but a school where only Jewish children went and only Jewish teachers taught. We were taught the usual things, of course, but also a few very important things which are not normally taught. First, when we came into class in the morning, the teacher would check that we all had a yellow star. If a child did not have one, they had to borrow a sweater or some other garment from another child. That was illegal, but at least everybody wore a star. The next lesson was: "What would you say if a soldier came into the class and asked you at what time your parents came home last night?" The answer had to be 'before 8.00 p.m.' (curfew hour) of course, but not too close to it. Something like 7.30 p.m. or 6.15 p.m., so that it would sound like the truth.

As Jews, we were not allowed to go to the movies or the public swimming pool, sit on park benches, play in the park, own radios, shop at any time except between three and five o'clock in the afternoon, go to plays, concerts or even the circus. We were not allowed to use public transit. Jewish men lost their jobs; they were not allowed to be journalists, symphony conductors, doctors, lawyers and many other professions. And of course we also had the curfew, as mentioned. We were not allowed to be out on the street between eight o'clock at night and six o'clock in the morning.

A number of our friends and acquaintances, fearing for their lives, went into hiding, though, as a child, I did not know that. For me people just 'disappeared', I did not know what had happened to them and nobody explained anything to me. A number of my friends vanished from school, but the teacher never explained that or said anything about it. These people just suddenly were gone.

My family did not go into hiding. After the war, my father told me that we had had the opportunity to do so but only if our family had been willing to separate. He told me that he had not wanted that, that he had thought that we should all stay together, so that we would either live or die together.

On June 20, 1943, when I had just turned ten years old, there was a big round-up in all of Amsterdam. The Germans came at about nine o'clock in the morning and chased us out of our apartment and down to the street. Many people were standing in the street and hanging out of windows, watching what was going on. Not everybody was hostile though. I remember clearly how Mrs. Gijtenbeek, the lady who owned the corner grocery store came to me with a small bag in her hand. In the bag were sweets that she wanted to give me. She had always been very nice to the neighborhood children and after the invasion she was even nicer to me than before.

We were taken to one of the big squares in Amsterdam and there we were made to wait. For what? We didn't know. We waited all morning. Finally, at about noon, we were taken to Central Station in Amsterdam. There, we were shoved into the cattle cars, packed in so tight that there was hardly room to breathe. We arrived in Westerbork, a concentration camp in the northeast of Holland, at about eleven o'clock at night and were sent through the wooden gates to one of the barracks where we had to register and undergo a medical examination. Then we were assigned to a barracks.

The barracks in Westerbork were long and low, ill-made of wood and with two dormitories for about 300 people each; men and boys over twelve years old in one room, women, girls and small boys in the other. Each of the two rooms was on one side of a sort of hallway. Our barracks was number 65. There were bunk beds, three tiers high, made of metal. They held a straw mattress and a straw pillow. There were no sheets and I was lucky that we had brought a blanket from home. There were not enough beds for everyone, so people had to share. I shared with my mother and grandmother. That was fortunate too, because I did not have to share with strangers, as so many others had to. We had two beds for the three of us.

All adults had to work. My father was assigned to the 'metal industry' where he had to flatten big metal pipes (like sewer pipes) with a huge hammer and my mother was assigned to a place where she had to tear apart batteries which were, I think, to be used in some war industry.

Food was brought to the barracks in Westerbork, on small wagons or carts, pulled by two men who also then ladled out the portions. These portions were far too small and of very bad quality. We all lost a lot of weight. We didn't look like the people one sees in pictures of Auschwitz, but we were severely underweight. Children did not have to work in Westerbork, so we mostly ran around doing nothing and getting in the way of the adults. There were no schools or other learning opportunities when I was there, except for learning how to steal food and other things which we might be able to barter for food.

Six months after our arrival in Westerbork, in January of 1944, we were deported to a concentration camp in what was then Czechoslovakia (now the Czech Republic). It was called Theresienstadt, the Czech name is Terezin. That trip took us two days in cattle cars. Again, we were housed in barracks, this time built out of stone. Theresienstadt was an old garrison town, built in 1780, for about 7000 soldiers and their families. The barracks were square, with a sort of small outside yard in the middle of the square. In the center of that yard stood a hand pump where we got our water. There were washrooms, but the water there was turned off for several hours every day. The water was rusty and smelled bad. Theresienstadt sits on marshy ground and the water came from the marsh.

Again men and women were separated. My father slept in a room for men, my mother and I in a room for women. Each room held about fifty people, though in the soldiers' time, they had probably held ten or fifteen men. Theresienstadt was, as mentioned, a small town. Although the soldiers and their families numbered only about seven thousand, we inmates, in my time there, numbered sixty thousand and therefore everything was vastly overcrowded. People who could not find beds, slept on the floors between the beds, in the halls, on the street, wherever they could find a spot.

Again, as in Westerbork, my parents had to work. My father's first job was as a street cleaner with a cart, a shovel and a broom made of twigs. He would sweep up the dirt and debris with the broom and toss it into the cart with the shovel. After the war, he often joked that that was the easiest job he had ever had and, besides, he had had wonderful, philosophical conversations with Rabbi Leo Baeck who worked with him as a street cleaner. Later, because he had been a pharmacist in his regular life, he worked in what was called the pharmacy, though there were no medications available. All there was, was some aspirin which people had had in their luggage, and very little of that.

My mother's first job was as part of a cleaning crew, not for us inmates, of course, but for the German headquarters in Theresienstadt. The headquarters were in what had been the town hall before the war. Some Germans just came there to work in their offices, but others were actually quartered there. Later, my mother was assigned to the mica factory, where only women worked. Mica is a mineral which looks somewhat like clear plastic. It is found in chunks which have layers that had to be split apart with an instrument that looked like a dull knife. Many years after the war, I learned that the mica was used in electronic war-equipment. Splitting it produced dust and many years later, my mother, like so many other women who had worked in the mica factory, died of lung problems.

Beginning in October of 1944, all children aged ten years and over, also had to work. My first job was as a message carrier for the Siechenhaus, the house for the old and sick. That was my 'regular' job. I was also assigned to a number of other jobs, one of which was passing cardboard boxes from one child to another, to a third, and so on, in a line. Only children were assigned to this particular work. Our line led from the crematorium to a waiting truck - though I didn't know that then. The boxes contained the ashes of the dead. The dead could not be buried, because as a result of the marshy ground, water would seep into the graves. So they were cremated. We children knew that full well, because we knew pretty much everything that went on and also because the boxes were ill-made and their covers did not quite fit. Ashes and bits of bone would seep out. The boxes had names on them as well, though I did not and do not know why. The waiting truck eventually went to the river Eger which flows past Theresienstadt and there the ashes were dumped into the river. I did not find this out, however, until many decades later.

Hunger, fear, illness and death ruled Theresienstadt at all times. In the autumn of 1944, two huge transports left Theresienstadt for the East. As I now know, but did not know then, they went to Auschwitz. The people in those transports were never heard from again.

On May 8, 1945, Theresienstadt was 'liberated' by the Russians who were on their way to somewhere else and happened upon Theresienstadt. This was the way in which most concentration camps were 'liberated'.

But what liberty? Who knew what we would find when we returned home or searched for relatives and friends? Who knew whether we would find any of our possessions? Mostly we found nobody and nothing; all family and friends had been murdered in the death camps. My family and I had to stay in Theresienstadt until late June of 1945. There was a typhus epidemic raging and, in order to avoid spreading the disease all over Europe, nobody was allowed to leave. Some inmates who hailed from Czechoslovakia left anyway; they either walked home or found a ride on some tank or with some car, but most of us could not leave.

After the epidemic was over, we were taken back to Holland, to Eindhoven, where we were temporarily quartered in the - then empty - Philips factories.

Eventually, on June 25, 1945, we were taken, by truck, back to Amsterdam, back to Central Station. There we learned that our pre-war upstairs neighbors, the Van den Berg family (mother Trien, father Wim, and their two daughters, the elder daughter Willy, and the younger one, my best friend Carla), had left word that, should we come back, they would take us in. So that's where we went. We stayed with them for about a year. After that year, we were able to rent the same apartment that we had had before the war. I had just turned twelve after liberation and I had to go back to elementary school where I was put in fifth grade. My father went back to work and life became 'normal' again. Only, of course, life was never normal again!

I could never talk to my parents about the war and the years in the camps. I could never ask questions about the people who had disappeared. Many of us, children and adults alike, could never talk about what had happened to us. We could not ask questions. We could not discuss it. People did not want to hear about it. Nobody wanted to listen. It was, and often still is, the 'great silence'.

We all had and have too many scars, both psychologically and physically. Most of us survivors have them. For us the war will never be over.

Memories of Neuengamme Concentration Camp

Loes de Kater

I was born in Amsterdam in 1938. This is a true story about my sister and me spending the last part of World War II in Neuengamme Concentration Camp in Germany. This story gives the first-hand account of two small witnesses who were there and suffered horrifying experiences. This is an educational and personal story about the Holocaust that should not be forgotten or discredited.

THE PROMISE

I listened to her labored breathing, her pain was very bad. The morphine drip was turned all the way open and running continuously. The cancer was on a rampage and devouring her body. She had courageously fought it for three years, but the disease had won the battle.

She wanted to tell me something, I came closer to her to hear what she was saying. "Do you need anything, Annie?" I asked.

"No, I want to talk to you, Loesje," she said. "Save your strength," I told her. "What for?" she replied with a smile. For a brief moment I saw my sister as she had been during her lifetime, strong and funny. "I am dying," she went on, "I don't need any more strength."

"So what can I get for you," I asked. She took a labored breath. "Loes, you have to write it all down."

"What do you want me to write down?" I asked her.

"About the camp," she said, "about what we went

through. About the Holocaust."

I looked at the remnants of my older sister. There was not much left of that once strong and vibrant woman. What the concentration camp had been unable to do, the cancer had achieved. It triumphed and brought down this tower of strength.

"You have to write it all down, about the concentration camp and how we survived. All that you remember and all that I remember."

"I do not write Annie," I objected. "You have to do this, Loes," she said, "otherwise we suffered for nothing." She gasped for air and closed her eyes. I did not want to upset her, so I told her: "Yes Annie, I will do it. I will write it all down."

Shortly after that conversation my sister died. It was a very sad time, it was like a part of me was gone. And I did not think about the promise that I made her.

But a little voice in my head started getting louder. It was my sister's voice. "You promised me, Loes," it said. So I picked up a pencil and paper, found a pleasant corner in my garden and started to write. The memories came flooding back. It was kind of comforting, like meeting an old friend I had not thought about for a long time. The words appeared on the paper as if by magic. Once I had started, I could not stop.

I have always had nightmares and have visited several doctors. I was diagnosed with Post Traumatic Stress Syndrome. I was prescribed several different medications for this, but I did not like how they made me feel, so I threw away the pills and learned to live with it. A strange thing happened. When I started to write down this story about the camp and our lives while we were there my nightmares became less and

I am less reluctant to talk about my experiences now. I still hear my sister's voice, but only to remind me of certain incidents and to push me to pick up my pencil again and continue writing when I come to a hurdle and stop.

So this story, this memory, is dedicated to my sister Annie, who took care of me in the concentration camp and saved my life and whose voice I still hear, saying "good job, Loes!"

OUR STORY

It was in the winter of 1944. A full moon lit up the landscape, the train rumbled through the white countryside. My sister and I huddled together trying to get warm. Shivering under an old worn blanket we talked quietly. "Don't be afraid," Annie said, "I will always take care of you."

We had been picked up off our Amsterdam street, the two of us, Annie, thirteen years old and I, Loes, almost six. I do not know to this day exactly why we were sent away to Neuengamme. We lived in Amsterdam's Jewish neighborhood. My father, a merchant seaman, who had been on duty in the Indies when the war in Europe started was away somewhere on the high seas, doing his bit for the war effort. He was Jewish. My mother was not, but she had been active in the Resistance and had been caught and locked up. It may have been because we were half-Jewish, or because mother was a resistance fighter, or both, but the reason why we were transported is immaterial. What happened to us after we were cruelly torn away from what remained of our family in Amsterdam is what this story is about.

The sudden noise of airplanes stopped my sister from

talking. She held me and pulled the blanket tightly over our heads. The noise suddenly became terribly loud. We screamed. The train rocked from side to side every time it was hit by a blast of machine gun fire. As suddenly as it had started it stopped again. We stopped screaming, like we were holding our breath. The train was still moving, slowly it moved to a side track and then stopped.

We heard harsh male voices speaking German. We came from under the blanket, our eyes large with fright. The bodies of several other children in our carriage were lying in pools of blood. The German soldiers carried them out of the train and laid them in an orderly row against the embankment of the railroad tracks. I went over to the sliding door of the carriage, now open, and stared out.

Much later, when I remembered the attack on the train, I would see a beautiful sight, like a painting, the red blood against the white snow and the full moon giving it all an eerie sparkle. "Loes, come here!" my sister called. I went back and crawled under the protective arms of my older sister.

The train started back up again after all the dead children had been carried out. The doors were closed and the two of us were back under the blanket, holding on to each other tightly. We were told later that the Allies bombed and shot at everything that moved and that since most trains in the last year and a half of the war were either troop or supply trains that mainly ran at night they believed we were a legitimate target. Since it was full moon that night the flyers could see our train clearly.

It was daylight now and the train once again came to

a halt. The doors were yanked open. We had to jump down onto the ground and were gathered up by the SS. They were constantly screaming orders. We were marched to a shed that was like a distribution center. It was very cold. There was a potbelly stove in the shed that gave the illusion of warmth, but since there were large openings in the wooden walls that was all it was: just an illusion. It was just as cold inside as outside. We were told which soldier to follow.

The two of us followed other kids down a road. There was a large stone building on our left side. After we passed through a gate there was a smaller wooden barrack on the left and at the end of the road was an open space where roll-calls were held. There were two more wooden barracks on the right and three more on the left. The kitchen was at the end, straight ahead. Music was playing. We looked for where it came from and we saw a group of prisoners playing instruments. They played very well. Later we found out that the longer they played, the longer they would stay alive. They gave several concerts, which kept the SS very happy. Hearing the beautiful music in that place was really ironic, because the smell of death and disease was all around us. It was so bad we could almost taste it.

We got to a certain barrack and a guard looked at our tags and told us to get inside it. The building did not look too bad from the outside, but when we walked in the stench was overwhelming. We both started to gag and held our noses, looking for bunks to sleep on. Prisoners with dead eyes and half-dead bodies lay listlessly in their bunks. A woman came towards us. "I have a bunk for you," she said. We did not know it yet, but this woman would be our protector. She told us how to stay away from trouble, when roll-call was and where. She showed us how to stay alive. The two of us had some experience in surviving on our own, we had been doing that in Amsterdam for some time, but we had never had to do it in concentration camp surroundings. The woman's name, we discovered later, was Evie Steinberg.

My sister was put to work at some of the factories and houses near the camp in cleaning details. This was not too bad, since she could steal some food or other items when she was cleaning the houses. She would be shot if the SS caught her, but it is what kept me alive. I would curl up in my bunk waiting for my sister to come back. My sister would always have something to eat. We did not have to wear the standard striped clothes and sometimes she would bring back some rags for us to wear. My sister took care of me, which in a way kept her going. She could not think too much about herself or the way we were living. She took everything the way it came and handled whatever came along. First thing in the morning before roll-call she would wash my face and made sure she was first in line for whatever meager portion of food was given to the prisoners. She would feed me and tell me to stay pretty much hidden until she returned from work detail.

One night Annie did not come back. It was already after roll-call and I started to cry softly. Evie came over to me and asked what was the matter. "I am afraid they killed my sister," I whimpered. "Be still," she said, "I will see what I can do." She went to the barrack door and peered outside into the darkness. "I am afraid to go outside, they will shoot me," she told me. Suddenly the door was thrown wide open and my sister was pushed inside. Her clothes were torn and she was bleeding. Evie knew right away what had happened. "Are you alright?" she asked Annie, "at least they did not kill you." She cleaned her up as well as she could and Annie and I crawled close to each other to get some warmth and some safety.

Annie was raped several times during our stay in Neuengamme. She did not get pregnant, she had never had a period yet. Many girls did not get periods because of malnutrition, especially in concentration camps.

The winter of 1944 felt like one of the coldest in centuries, or maybe it just seemed that way to us. The cold wind howled around the camp. There was no heat in our barrack, so the two of us and Evie huddled under our old blanket and coats to keep warm. I remember some of our conversations: "I never want to be cold again," said Annie. "As soon as we get out of here I will go to a warm land."

"You are so right," Evie agreed. And that is what they did. Evie moved to Spain after the war and my sister Annie died in Florida, with me at her side.

Prisoners around us were dying at a record pace. The main cause of death was dysentery. There was no medical care, although there were several doctors at the camp. The prisoners were not looked after. Lack of food, hard work and unsanitary conditions killed most of the prisoners.

Later, when I was grown, my reoccurring nightmare was always about standing on a table, my head shaved and my entire body covered in sulfur, with the exception of my eyes with men in white coats looking up at me. I would always have that flashback whenever I smelled sulfur like when a match was struck. I always thought this was done to treat scurvy, which I may have had. Just another nightmare, I thought. But later, when I did some research on what happened in Neuengamme I discovered that medical experiments involving sulfur had taken place there.

We were constantly beaten and interrogated with questions about my mother being in the Resistance. Both of us remembered our mother reaching across the partition between our back yard and our neighbors'. She grasped the baby that was handed to her by the young mother who lived next door. We heard the sound of a front door being broken down by the Gestapo, very loudly. Orders were shouted as the young mother turned back and walked back into her house. We never saw the young mother again, but the baby was brought to a safe place and survived.

There was also the time that my mother draped a tapestry in front of the shower door, where she was hiding two Allied pilots. We knew that she was helping people, but were told over and over again not to say anything if anyone ever asked about it. But we were not told very much in case the Gestapo would get a hold of us.

When I was interrogated and the beatings would go on and on I would go to another place. I could not feel or hear the guards hitting me. To this day I still have a four inch scar on my head where the hair will not grow. I never knew where the scar came from, until my sister told me that I was being questioned by one of the guards. I did not answer the questions fast enough, the guard got impatient and he hit me with the butt of his rifle on the side of my head.

Children will block trauma or pain. It is a defensive mechanism that will spare their sanity so that in later life they will not remember. But the memories will come out in their dreams.

Both Annie and I suffered for the rest of our lives from severe stomach and intestinal problems. We believe this was caused by our stay in the camp. One of the camp doctors performed an experiment testing a new water filter in the winter of 1944-1945 by adding 100 times the safe dose of arsenic to water. He gave it to more than 150 prisoners, which caused long term injury to most of them. Maybe we were part of the experiment.

One vivid recurring dream was about white buses. The dream came back again and again. Later I discovered that the white buses had been used to evacuate Scandinavian prisoners to neutral Sweden. We were told the prisoners on the white buses were being taken to death camps, so they represented danger in our minds, but in reality they saved the lives of several thousand prisoners.

One Dutch camp guard who came from Amsterdam, just like us was befriended by my sister. He would bring us some food and on occasion some clothing.

Our meals usually consisted of turnip soup and a crust of bread. My sister would always feed me before she would eat herself. Often she would not have enough for both of us and she would go hungry. Sometimes we had to hide the food that Annie brought back. There were lots of hungry prisoners in our barrack and some would kill for a scrap of food. We would share our food with Evie, who would in turn share what she had and protect us and our hidden food, when we had it. In the time that we were in Neuengamme a strong bond developed between us and Evie.

On November 21, 1944 Annie woke me. "Loes, it is your birthday," she whispered. "How do you know that?" I asked. "I saw a calendar in one of the houses I cleaned," she replied. Evie was awake too. "We have to do something," she said. "She is turning six," Annie told Evie and pulled a blue ribbon from underneath the rags that covered her thin body. My favorite color was blue. "I have no hair to put it in," I cried softly. The Germans had shaved off all my hair. "We can put it around your neck," Annie said.

One night when Annie and I were huddled together, I remember, we were trying to sleep, but the stench of death and disease was so overwhelming, it kept us awake. The lonely distant sound of a train blowing its whistle rippled the stillness of the night. I asked my sister softly: "is it always going to be like this, Annie?" "I don't know, Loesje," she said, "we will get out of here, I promise."

A gentle rain was falling on the metal roof of the barrack where we slept. Annie shook me softly. "It is spring," she whispered. I tried to open my eyes and look at my older sister. "Oh Annie, is it going to warm up? The flowers will come out, we won't be so cold, maybe we will go home." "It will not matter," Annie said, " I will take care of you, even if we have to stay here." She hugged me firmly.

During this time the bombing of nearby Hamburg became ever more frequent and intense. The city was under attack day and night. Prisoners were sent into the city to help dig out people who were buried under homes and buildings. Every evening these prisoners would come back to the camp in dismay. They would tell us about the screaming from basements where people were trapped. 'The whole world is on fire,' they would say.

In March of 1945 there was a lot of commotion. We asked Evie what was going on. "The SS is moving all the prisoners out," she said. "Where to?" Annie asked. "To the death camps," Evie answered. Annie let out a small moan. She said: "we will be next." Evie advised her to talk to the Dutch guard. She waited for the guard to come on duty. As soon as she saw him she walked over to him. "Keep walking," he said to her softly, "act like I am taking you somewhere." The two of them walked over to behind the kitchen. If anyone saw them the guard could say she was cleaning the garbage cans, not that anyone was paying much attention. The guards were too busy gathering up all the Jewish prisoners to move them into trains and buses.

"I already know what you are going to say," the guard told my sister. "I have a small suitcase for you, with food in it and some clothing. I am going to let you out tomorrow immediately after roll-call. The count is not accurate anymore anyway, most prisoners are already gone. They are only keeping some here to burn all the records."

That evening the guard brought us our clothing. It was nothing fancy, we were not supposed to be noticed, but it was better than the tattered rags we had been wearing. We could not look like we had just come out of a concentration camp. That was a bit of a challenge. We were so thin, our cheeks so sunken and Annie was infected with tuberculosis and coughing so hard that her chest would cave in.

The next morning Annie dressed me with clothes the guard had given me. We hugged Evie and promised to get in touch with her after the war. (Annie did that, she finally tracked her down in 1995 and found out that she was living in Spain. She contacted Evie, who sent her a video tape of herself with a message for us.) Most prisoners walked slowly towards the area where we had to be counted. The SS counted sloppily, not paying much attention to who was there or not, they just wanted to get it over with and get away.

Right after the count was over Annie and I walked toward the entrance of the camp. It was wide open. Guards were shoving people into buses and marching them down the road. Suddenly a hand reached out and pulled Annie to the side of the wooden barrack. "Come!" the Dutch guard whispered. He took us behind the building. "There is an opening in the fence," he told Annie. "Here is the suitcase. You will have to stay off the road, or they'll pick you up again."

We climbed through the opening in the fence and moved away from the camp as fast as we could. Annie was coughing, her face was ashen because of the tuberculosis that she had run up in the camp. But she was a strong girl and that was her survival. We kept walking and got off the main road, following the advice of the Dutch guard. We walked down dirt roads as fast as we could. Annie had learned to speak German fluently in the camp. When someone asked why we were walking there, she would say that we were visiting family and that the trains had stopped running. The farmers did not suspect us and let us sleep in their barns, sometimes even gave us a ride on a hay wagon. Bombing was still fierce, the Allies were going all out.

As we got close to the Dutch border we crossed a bridge that was being patrolled by German soldiers. They asked us where we were from and Annie told them too that we were visiting relatives. The soldiers believed her and told us to hurry across because they were going to blow up the bridge so the Allies could not use it. We walked across the bridge. There was an eerie stillness as we reached the other side. The birds did not chirp and the leaves did not move. Suddenly we saw a helmet come from between the bushes and then some more popped up. Soon there were a dozen or so. The helmets did not belong to German uniforms. One of the soldiers spoke, in a nice sounding rolling sort of way. We did not understand a word, just stared at these strange looking men. Finally using hand gestures that we understood the men asked us if there were German soldiers on the bridge. We said 'yes' and tried to tell the men that the Germans were about to blow up the bridge. But the strange looking men did not understand us. They gestured us to move along. We had not gone far when we heard rapid gunfire and then a terrible explosion. We knew what had happened and did not look back, but continued on our journey.

The journey was getting very draining on both of us. We walked slower and slower and often had to take a detour, because a lot of roads were so severely bombed that they could not be used. The one thing that kept us going was the thought that there would still be some family left in Amsterdam.

The small suitcase was almost empty. I was softly whimpering: "I am hungry Annie." "Just hold on a little bit longer, we will be home soon," my sister said. Then she took the last piece of black German bread out and gave it to me. "There still is some cheese and sausage left," she told me, "but we have to keep that for later." We tried to get some milk at farmhouses that we passed. Sometimes we were lucky, but usually we were chased off. Occasionally Annie had to agree to exchange sexual favors for a small amount of milk. She did not complain, it was survival.

There were lines of German soldiers walking the opposite way. The men looked haggard and defeated. A horse went through its knees and fell. It was pushed to the side of the road. There were a lot of bicycles being pushed and ridden. Most of these had been confiscated in Holland. We looked at the men with their hollow eyes and walked in the opposite direction towards Amsterdam.

When we got to IJssel Lake we knew we were close. There was a boat going across to Amsterdam. The skipper agreed to take us. Annie was now very sick from the tuberculosis. She was coughing, her frame heaved and she started to spit up blood.

We walked down the old street where we used to live. It was in the old Jewish section of Amsterdam and every house was in ruins, except one house, our house, number 15. We walked up to the front door. It was still hanging on one hinge, it had been kicked in so many times that it had finally collapsed. We crawled in through the opening. The house looked abandoned, most of the cabinets in the kitchen had been ripped out for firewood, part of the floor was also gone. We found some sort of couch and sat down. Annie had a hard time breathing. "I will look for food," I said. "Is there any food left in the suitcase?" "No," Annie answered. She was too sick to get up and look, so I started to look around. It looked like other people had gone through the place already. All there was, was some broken pottery. Suddenly I heard a scraping noise. I ran to where my older sister was slumped down. I grabbed her and we held on to each other, our eyes large with fright as a large shadow moved across the room toward us. The setting sun made it look even larger. We closed our eyes, tightly gripping each other when suddenly we heard a scream. We opened our eyes and saw our older sister Mientje standing in what was once the doorway. For the longest time we just stared at each other. And then Mientje asked so many questions, we did not know what to answer, we were so relieved to see our older sister. We all started to cry.

Mientje told us that the family did not know what had happened to us and thought that we were dead. My mother had been tortured so badly that she was still in the hospital, my brother had been taken away to perform slave labor in North Africa for the Germans.

Mientje had some food and the first thing she did was to feed us and to try to arrange a place for us to sleep. The next day she took both of us to the hospital where our mother was and had Annie examined. Luckily the tuberculosis was still treatable and with medical attention and drugs from the US Army she eventually recovered. Mientje went to work fixing the doors and making dresses and coats from old army blankets that she had stolen. She used an old sewing machine that we had found. We saw mother in the hospital. She was in very bad shape after her treatment by the Gestapo, but it was a happy reunion, the hardships were gone, the country was free and the war was over.

But there were a lot of children damaged by the war. Some of these were brought to recuperation centers. I was sent to such a place too. This was the first time I was given a tooth brush and a bar of soap, Palmolive soap. We were given cod liver oil and then some licorice to hide the taste. I was only in the center for six weeks. Not much, to regain strength after years of hunger and neglect.

After that I was sent home again. But our home was not what you would call a place for young children to grow up in. There was no money, most of the population had not been to school for some time and stealing was the order of the day. Annie and I were arrested for stealing and sent to an orphanage, where I was in constant fights with other kids. We were used to fighting for our food and that was when most of the fights broke out, during the meals. Where I should have been counseled I was sent instead to a reform institution. I was like a small wild animal, so I constantly ran away. I did not return home, but went instead to where my sister was kept. One time I hitch-hiked to Schiedam, where my sister was. It was dark when I got there. The gate to the institution, usually open, was locked tight. I wondered what I should do and walked to a nearby park. I crawled under some bushes and tried to sleep. I heard voices, drunken men coming from a bar that had just closed. The park was clearly not a safe place, so I decided to try the gate again, but it was still locked. So I climbed up the wall, which was hard, because there was broken glass on top to keep the children in. One of the caretakers saw me and carefully got me down.

Many years later when I was sixteen I was at a restaurant with some of my friends. There were some American officers sitting at another table. One of them kept staring at me. Eventually he came over and introduced himself. Little did I know then that I would fall madly in love, be married within a year and be widowed within three years. He was an American fighter pilot and his plane crashed right after we moved to the United States.

Both Annie and I married at a very young age and left the country, trying to get away from the bad memories of war and its after effects. What we were not aware of then, is that we would always carry those memories with us.

Contributors

Christina Sobole-van der Kroon
Christina Sobole-van der Kroon was born in Limburg. When she was three years old the family (six girls and a boy) moved to Amsterdam.

Early in the war the family and its business were forcibly relocated, because the house they occupied obstructed the view of the German sea planes moored at the docks. They moved to Waterloo Square (Waterlooplein), the center of the Jewish district.

In 1957 Christine came to Canada alone. She met her future husband in Montreal. Christine lived in San Francisco, New York City and Seattle. In California she got a college degree in Music and Recreational Therapy. She retired with her husband in Las Vegas.

Anne Bourne
Anne Bourne lives in Fairfax, California.

Art van Leeuwen
Art van Leeuwen came to Canada after the war, where he worked as an electrician. He lives in Whitby, Ontario.

Anthonia Huysman
Anthonia Huysman was seven years old when the war started and lived in Groningen. She came to the USA with her parents in 1948. She has a son and a daughter and two grandchildren and lives in Buena Park, California.

Wim Bongers
Wim Bongers was born in Hoorn in 1933. He came to

Canada in 1952. He had a long career with Nortel in Toronto and Montreal. In 1991 he retired in Bathurst, New Brunswick, where he still lives with his wife.

Olga Chesbrough
Olga Chesbrough lives in Venice, Florida.

Liesbeth Boysen-van den Blink
Liesbeth was ten years old and lived in Eindhoven at the start of the war. After a marriage of 58 years with her husband Mike, also from Eindhoven, she passed away in April of 2011 after a short illness. She lived in Bobcaygeon, Ontario.

Jerry Meents
Jerry was nine years old when the Germans invaded Holland. Jerry's father was Jewish, his mother was not. The family lived in Amsterdam in the Transvaal-neighborhood, which had a large Jewish population. He fought in the Israeli war of independence in 1948-49, but returned to Amsterdam afterward. In 1957 he came to the USA with his wife, his seven year old son and $1.25 in his pocket. He settled in Ogden, Utah, where he still lives.

Truus Leader
Truus married her first husband, an American, in Amsterdam and then moved to California in 1956. They had two children. After her first husband passed away she remarried and she has been together with her current husband for 32 years now. Truus has always been deeply grateful to the Allied soldiers that liberated The Netherlands. She became a member and president

of the American Legion Auxiliary in Napoleon, Ohio, where she still lives.

Jan de Zwager

Jan was eight years old when the war started and lived in Haarlem, the oldest child in a large growing family. After the war he worked for Bruynzeel, where in the 1960s he set up a door factory and was responsible for the acquisition and management of several other door factories.

In 1985 he retired in the south of France, in the département of Gers, where he still lives. As the oldest of ten children Jan's memories of the war were most vivid and he often told his siblings snippets of them. His sister Carla, who lives in Canada, asked him to write down his memories, which he did.

Jaap Matz

Jaap followed his brother Bernard to Israel in 1952, where he became an English teacher. After his retirement in 1995 he started tutoring students at a local elementary school who had trouble with English. He still does that. Jaap is very happily married and has ten grandchildren. He lives in Kyriat Motzkin in Israel.

Rita Binder

Rita grew up in Stadskanaal in the province of Groningen and moved with her family to Gouda before the war when she was 14 years old. She lived in Gouda during the war. She came to Canada on her own in the late 1940s, where she met her husband. Rita has five children and six grandchildren and lives in Wahnapitae near Sudbury in Ontario.

Hetty Wear

Hetty was 21 in 1946 when she married a Canadian soldier, John Wear. She met him shortly after the end of the war and joined him in Edmonton, Alberta where she still lives. She has a daughter and two sons and several grandchildren and great-grandchildren. She worked for Woodwards and Sears department stores after the kids had grown up. Her husband died in 1999. Each month Hetty still attends a gathering of Edmonton war-brides.

Sjenta Wilkinson

Sjenta came to Canada in 1953 with her family. They settled in Kelowna, British Columbia, where they ran a show garden. After moving to Vancouver some years later Sjenta qualified as a Practical Nurse. She remarried after her husband passed away. Sjenta still loves to go sailing on Okanagan lake near Kelowna, where she lived for many years. Widowed again, she now lives in White Rock, British Columbia.

Ruth Gabriele Sarah Silten

Ruth Silten came to California in 1959 to visit friends of her parents. She stayed and still lives in California, in Pomona.

Loes de Kater

Loes was born in Amsterdam in 1938 to a Jewish father and a non-Jewish mother. When she was almost six she was sent to Neuengamme concentration camp with her older sister. After the war she met her future husband, an American pilot, in Amsterdam. She moved to the USA with him in 1956. Within three years of their wedding he crashed his plane and she was widowed. Loes lives in Casselberry, Florida.

The Dutch in Wartime series

Book 1
Invasion

Edited by:
Tom Bijvoet

90 pages paperback
ISBN: 978-0-9868308-0-8

Book 2
Under Nazi Rule

Edited by:
Tom Bijvoet

88 pages paperback
ISBN: 978-0-9868308-3-9

Book 3
Witnessing the Holocaust

Edited by:
Tom Bijvoet

96 pages paperback
ISBN: 978-0-9868308-5-3

Book 4
Resisting Nazi Occupation

Edited by:
Anne van Arragon Hutten

108 pages paperback
ISBN: 978-0-9868308-4-6

Book 5
Tell your children about us

Edited by:
Anne van Arragon Hutten

104 pages paperback
ISBN: 978-0-9868308-6-0

Book 6
War in the Indies

Edited by:
Anne van Arragon Hutten

96 pages paperback
ISBN: 978-0-9868308-7-7

Book 7
Caught in the crossfire

Edited by:
Anne van Arragon Hutten

104 pages paperback
ISBN: 978-0-9868308-8-4

Book 8
The Hunger Winter

Edited by:
Tom Bijvoet &
Anne van Arragon Hutten

110 pages paperback
ISBN: 978-0-9868308-9-1

Book 9
Liberation

Edited by:
Anne van Arragon Hutten

114 pages paperback
ISBN: 978-0-9919981-0-4

Keep your series complete: order on-line at mokeham.com or contact Mokeham Publishing.

CPSIA information can be obtained at www.ICGtesting.com
Printed in the USA
BVOW08s1007231113

337045BV00002B/4/P